A STRONG AND COURAGEOUS CHURCH

Advancing God's Kingdom through Discipleship and Leadership Development

Copyright © 2016, World Impact, Inc. All Rights Reserved

Scripture quotations marked ESV are from The Holy Bible, English Standard Version® (ESV®), copyright © 2001 by Crossway, a publishing ministry of Good News Publishers. All rights reserved.

All resources marked TUMI are from The Urban Ministry Institute. Used by Permission. All rights reserved. www.tumi.org

CONTENTS

	Acknowledgements	5
	Introduction	7
1	**Counting the Cost:** Starting Well in Early Discipleship	13
2	**Over the Hump:** Equipping the Saints for the Work of the Ministry	37
3	**Fit to Represent:** The Next Generation of the Church	61
	Appendices	87

ACKNOWLEDGEMENTS

A Strong and Courageous Church is a road map of wisdom from the Bible, as well as many years of ministry experience, on what it means to make disciples in the city. We want to thank the faithful men and women who have contributed to this book both directly and indirectly.

Christ the Victor Church was birthed through the work of World Impact missionaries and church planters whose experiences and wisdom are reflected in this book. Their lessons learned and kingdom victories are invaluable to us and we appreciate the sacrifices they and their families have made to advance the kingdom in some of the hardest and darkest places. While our movement was built on the work that World Impact has done in the city for decades, it is carried on by our strong and courageous CTV pastors and leaders who are pouring into men and women and children in the city. These leaders are the heart of our movement and we are so thankful to serve along such wise and determined kingdom warriors.

The CTV Movement as a whole and this particular resource have been deeply influenced by the passion and work of Rev. Dr. Don L. Davis and we are grateful for the clarity with which he communicates biblical truth and how he and his team at The Urban Ministry Institute work tirelessly to create resources for urban leaders to use in the ministry field.

We would also like to acknowledge the work of CTV Head Bishop Rev. Daren Busenitz, Rev. Ryan Carter, and Adria Medlen for the many hours given to creating this resource and for the many people who lent us their eyes and wisdom to hone and edit the final product.

INTRODUCTION

A strong and courageous church is a disciple-making church. There is no other way.

The primary command of the Great Commission in Matthew's Gospel is "make disciples" (Matt 28.19). Discipleship is not a small matter for the church. It is not one among many things that we do. In some ways, discipleship is the sum of our life together. We follow Jesus as disciples and we evangelize, equip, and empower other disciples to be strong and courageous for the Lord.

Far too often our beliefs and practices about discipleship are misinformed by false models and desires. If we are truly to become strong and courageous disciple-making churches, we need to be set free from falsehood. At the outset of this resource, we would like to lay out four delusional desires that we need to be freed from if we truly want to see dynamic discipleship.

1. **There are no golden keys that will make discipleship fast and easy.**

    This is the lie that many discipleship books and curricula peddle. 'If you buy this book, you will find the 5 reliable steps to making mature disciples! In 6 months you can revolutionize your church!!!'

    Stop believing the sales pitch. There is no such thing. Discipleship will always remain *A Long Obedience in the Same Direction.*[1] We did not create this resource to make discipleship fast and easy. We created it to encourage you because discipleship is slow and difficult!

---

[1] Title of a wonderful book by Eugene Peterson (IVP, 2000).

2. **There are no experts in making disciples, but there is wisdom.**

   Being a disciple of Jesus involves our whole life, our whole being, and our whole sphere of existence in the world. Everything is included. Discipleship always and forever remains bound to the chaotic messiness of actual lives and families and relationships. If you have been married for any length of time, you understand how difficult it is to become an expert in another human being's life. How much less can we be experts in the lives of everyone who follows Christ!

   However, there is good wisdom that we can apply broadly as churches. What we represent in this resource is not our expertise, but the collective wisdom of many World Impact disciple-makers over the years.

3. **There is no substitute for the Holy Spirit.**

   It would be wonderful if there was some way to guarantee outcomes in discipleship. If only there was an equation of hours spent in prayer, number of Bible studies attended, counseling meetings, home visits, and service projects that would always produce the result of mature godly disciples!

   This, however, is a false hope. Anyone who has tried seriously to make disciples can tell you that guaranteeing results is impossible. The reason for this is that true transformation in the image of Jesus Christ always remains the work of the Holy Spirit. All attempts to usurp the Spirit's role and make transformation happen by our own ingenuity will fall short of true discipleship. Discipleship is not ultimately about you and what you do to someone. It is about pursuing God, and what he does in us all as we journey together.

4. **There is also no substitute for you.**

   While transformation is ultimately the work of the Holy Spirit, God has so ordained it that spiritual leaders would be an indispensable ingredient in the discipleship process.

Kevin DeYoung has said "The one indispensable requirement for producing godly, mature Christians is godly, mature Christians."[2] There is no program, no book, no curriculum, and no liturgy that can take the place of a godly leader. In other words, you cannot do effective discipleship on auto-pilot. You are important to the discipleship of your members. Not you as a program director, or even you as a preacher, but you as a disciple of Jesus. Our Lord has placed you in your context, and called you to walk with confidence into the disciple-making vision he has given you for the church.

My prayer for Christ the Victor is that we would be a dynamic disciple-making movement. If we truly want to see a rapid multiplication of churches in our cities, discipleship will have to be the engine that powers us there. Be strong and courageous!

Guiding Concepts

Throughout this book we will reference three important charts (see following charts on pages 10-12). The content of these, created by Dr. Don L. Davis from The Urban Ministry Institute, has informed and shaped our dialogue on discipleship and leadership development as discussed in this book:

---

[2] From *Reaching the Next Generation: Hold Them With Holiness*, blog post on October 21, 2009 (https://blogs.thegospelcoalition.org/kevindeyoung/2009/10/21/reaching-the-next-generation-hold-them-with-holiness/)

The Hump
Rev. Dr. Don L. Davis • 1Timothy 4.9-16; Hebrews 5.11-14

The Baby Christian
The New Believer and the Spiritual Disciplines

Awkwardness

Unskillfulness

Mistakes

Roughness

Sporadic Behavior

Uncomfortableness

Inefficiency

Novice-Level Performance

The Mature Christian
The Mature Believer and the Spiritual Disciplines

Faithful Application

Gracefulness

Automatic response

Comfortableness

Personal Satisfaction

Excellence

Expertise

Training Others

Heart Desire
A Clear Goal
Feasible Plan
Solid Support
Correct Knowledge
Faithful Effort
Good Examples
Extended Period of Time
Longsuffering

Regular, correct application of the spiritual disciplines

© 2004. The Urban Ministry Institute. All Rights Reserved. The Urban Ministry Institute is a ministry of World Impact, Inc.

Fit to Represent: Multiplying Disciples of the Kingdom of God
Rev. Dr. Don L. Davis

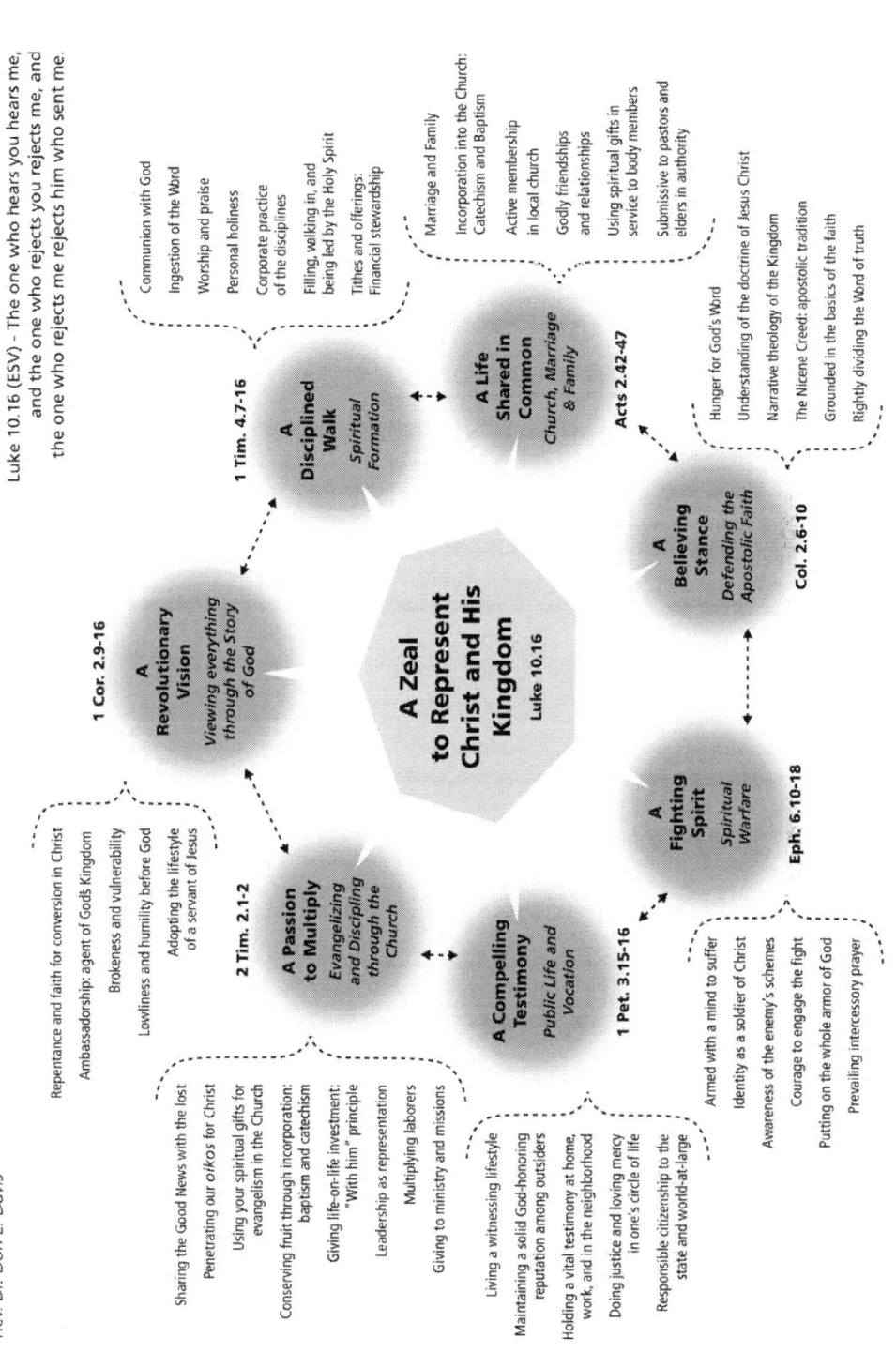

Luke 10.16 (ESV) - The one who hears you hears me, and the one who rejects you rejects me, and the one who rejects me rejects him who sent me.

A Zeal to Represent Christ and His Kingdom
Luke 10.16

A Disciplined Walk
Spiritual Formation
1 Tim. 4.7-16

- Communion with God
- Ingestion of the Word
- Worship and praise
- Personal holiness
- Corporate practice of the disciplines
- Filling, walking in, and being led by the Holy Spirit
- Tithes and offerings: Financial stewardship

A Life Shared in Common
Church, Marriage & Family
Acts 2.42-47

- Marriage and Family
- Incorporation into the Church: Catechism and Baptism
- Active membership in local church
- Godly friendships and relationships
- Using spiritual gifts in service to body members
- Submissive to pastors and elders in authority

A Believing Stance
Defending the Apostolic Faith
Col. 2.6-10

- Hunger for God's Word
- Understanding of the doctrine of Jesus Christ
- Narrative theology of the Kingdom
- The Nicene Creed: apostolic tradition
- Grounded in the basics of the faith
- Rightly dividing the Word of truth

A Fighting Spirit
Spiritual Warfare
Eph. 6.10-18

- Armed with a mind to suffer
- Identity as a soldier of Christ
- Awareness of the enemy's schemes
- Courage to engage the fight
- Putting on the whole armor of God
- Prevailing intercessory prayer

A Compelling Testimony
Public Life and Vocation
1 Pet. 3.15-16

- Living a witnessing lifestyle
- Maintaining a solid God-honoring reputation among outsiders
- Holding a vital testimony at home, work, and in the neighborhood
- Doing justice and loving mercy in one's circle of life
- Responsible citizenship to the state and world-at-large

A Passion to Multiply
Evangelizing and Discipling through the Church
2 Tim. 2.1-2

- Sharing the Good News with the lost
- Penetrating our *oikos* for Christ
- Using your spiritual gifts for evangelism in the Church
- Conserving fruit through incorporation: baptism and catechism
- Giving life-on-life investment: "With him" principle
- Leadership as representation
- Multiplying laborers
- Giving to ministry and missions

A Revolutionary Vision
Viewing everything through the Story of God
1 Cor. 2.9-16

- Repentance and faith for conversion in Christ
- Ambassadorship: agent of God's Kingdom
- Brokeness and vulnerability
- Lowliness and humility before God
- Adopting the lifestyle of a servant of Jesus

© 2002. The Urban Ministry Institute. All Rights Reserved. The Urban Ministry Institute is a ministry of World Impact, Inc.

Discerning the Call: The Profile of a Cross-Cultural Urban Church Planter
Rev. Dr. Don L. Davis

	Commission	Character	Community	Competence
Definition	Recognizes the call of God and replies with prompt obedience to his lordship and leading	Reflects the character of Christ in his/her personal convictions, conduct, and lifestyle	Regards multiplying disciples in the body of Christ as the primary role of ministry	Responds in the power of the Spirit with excellence in carrying out their appointed tasks and ministry
Key Scripture	2 Tim. 1.6-14; 1 Tim. 4.14; Acts 1.8; Matt. 28.18-20	John 15.4-5; 2 Tim. 2.2; 1 Cor. 4.2; Gal. 5.16-23	Eph. 4.9-15; 1 Cor. 12.1-27	2 Tim. 2.15; 3.16-17; Rom. 15.14; 1 Cor. 12
Critical Concept	The Authority of God: God's leader acts on God's recognized call and authority, acknowledged by the saints and God's leaders	The Humility of Christ: God's leader demonstrates the mind and lifestyle of Christ in his or her actions and relationships	The Growth of the Church: God's leader uses all of his or her resources to equip and empower the body of Christ for his/her goal and task	The Power of the Spirit: God's leader operates in the gifting and anointed of the Holy Spirit
Central Elements	A clear call from God Authentic testimony before God and others Deep sense of personal conviction based on Scripture Personal burden for a particular task or people Confirmation by leaders and the body	Passion for Christlikeness Radical lifestyle for the Kingdom Serious pursuit of holiness Discipline in the personal life Fulfills role-relationships and bond-slave of Jesus Christ Provides an attractive model for others in their conduct, speech, and lifestyle (the fruit of the Spirit)	Genuine love for and desire to serve God's people Disciples faithful individuals Facilitates growth in small groups Pastors and equips believers in the congregation Nurtures associations and networks among Christians and churches Advances new movements among God's people locally	Endowments and gifts from the Spirit Sound discipling from an able mentor Skill in the spiritual disciplines Ability in the Word Able to evangelize, follow up, and disciple new converts Strategic in the use of resources and people to accomplish God's task
Satanic Strategy to Abort	Operates on the basis of personality or position rather than on God's appointed call and ongoing authority	Substitutes ministry activity and/or hard work and industry for godliness and Christlikeness	Exalts tasks and activities above equipping the saints and developing Christian community	Functions on natural gifting and personal ingenuity rather than on the Spirit's leading and gifting
Key Steps	Identify God's call Discover your burden Be confirmed by leaders	Abide in Christ Discipline for godliness Pursue holiness in all	Embrace God's Church Learn leadership's contexts Equip concentrically	Discover the Spirit's gifts Receive excellent training Hone your performance
Results	Deep confidence in God arising from God's call	Powerful Christlike example provided for others to follow	Multiplying disciples in the Church	Dynamic working of the Holy Spirit

© 2002. The Urban Ministry Institute. All Rights Reserved. The Urban Ministry Institute is a ministry of World Impact, Inc.

§1

COUNTING THE COST

Starting Well in Early Discipleship

Joshua and The Golden Calf (Exodus 32.17, 33.11) – What is it really like to lead Israel?

Joshua, who was to be Moses' successor as the leaders of Israel, gets a foretaste of what it is truly like to lead this people. Exodus 24.13 says "So Moses rose with his assistant Joshua, and Moses went up into the mountain of God." As they are up on the mountain Aaron leads the people in the crafting and worship of a golden calf. Exodus 32.17 says, "When Joshua heard the noise of the people as they shouted, he said to Moses, 'There is a noise of war in the camp.'" After they descend and rebuke the people, Moses meets with the Lord in a tent outside the camp to intercede for the people. Exodus 33.11 notes, "Thus the LORD used to speak to Moses face to face, as a man speaks to his friend. When Moses turned again into the camp, his assistant Joshua the son of Nun, a young man, would not depart from the tent."

At every stage of the horrible golden calf incident, Joshua is present with Moses. He watches the pain and struggle of what Moses is doing. Joshua here has the opportunity to see clearly the dark side of his future leadership role. The Lord affords him this time to *count the cost* of being Israel's leader.

Counting the Cost

New believers need to be rooted in a clear sense of what it truly means to follow Christ. Just as Joshua saw both the hardships and the blessings of leading the Israelites through Moses' example, your disciples need a clear understanding of what they are stepping into. Our Lord affirms this in a remarkable text:

> [25] *Now great crowds accompanied him, and he turned and said to them,* [26] *"If anyone comes to me and does not hate his own father and mother and wife and children and brothers and sisters, yes, and even his own life, he cannot be my disciple.* [27] *Whoever does not bear his own cross and come after me cannot be my disciple.* [28] *For which of you, desiring to build a tower, does not* **first sit down and count the cost, whether he has enough to complete it?** [29] *Otherwise, when he has laid a foundation and is not able to finish, all who see it begin to mock him,* [30] *saying, 'This man began to build and was not able to finish.'* Luke 14.25–30 (ESV)

It is not our goal to simply help new believers begin the journey of discipleship. In the earliest stage of their journey, we want to do the necessary groundwork of nurture, care, instruction, and correction that will empower them to finish what they have started. In other words, we must help them count the cost of life in Christ.

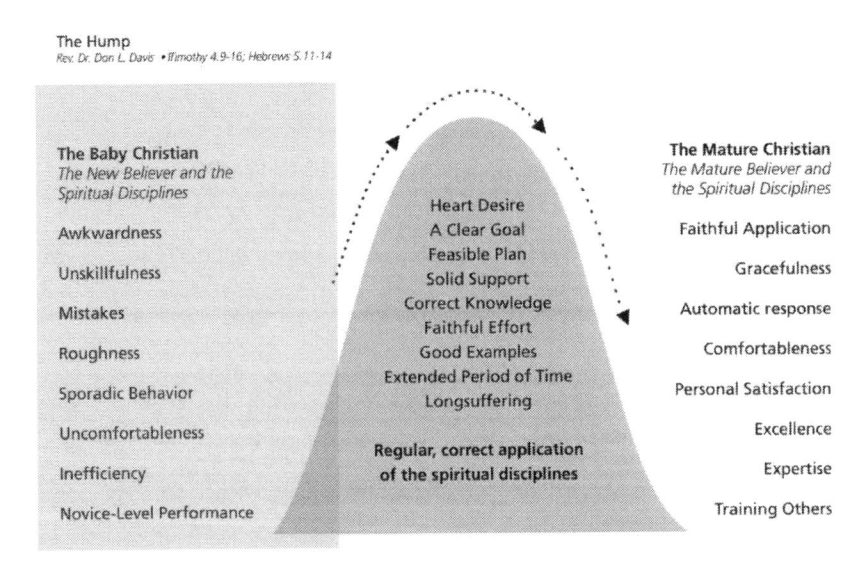

The Hump
Rev. Dr. Don L. Davis • 1 Timothy 4.9-16; Hebrews 5.11-14

The Baby Christian
The New Believer and the Spiritual Disciplines

Awkwardness

Unskillfulness

Mistakes

Roughness

Sporadic Behavior

Uncomfortableness

Inefficiency

Novice-Level Performance

Heart Desire
A Clear Goal
Feasible Plan
Solid Support
Correct Knowledge
Faithful Effort
Good Examples
Extended Period of Time
Longsuffering

Regular, correct application of the spiritual disciplines

The Mature Christian
The Mature Believer and the Spiritual Disciplines

Faithful Application

Gracefulness

Automatic response

Comfortableness

Personal Satisfaction

Excellence

Expertise

Training Others

© 2004. The Urban Ministry Institute. All Rights Reserved. The Urban Ministry Institute is a ministry of World Impact, Inc.

Counting the Cost: Starting Well in Early Discipleship

What does this look like?

The Church is God's Family

In the early stage of discipleship it is crucial to remember that we are the family of God. The key to incorporating a new believer into the church is welcoming them into the warmth of God's family. As you will see in this section, understanding this concept will lead to a healthy shared spirituality in your church and guide much of your discipleship process.

This is not just a concept for the new believer, but it is especially important for someone who is new to the faith or whose normal support system is dysfunctional and ungodly. Just as it is crucial for them to understand that they are breaking ties with who they used to be and leaving behind the ways of the world, it is also crucial for them to know that they are being welcomed *into* something. As they understand and take their place as children of God and brothers or sisters in Christ they can receive all the care and nurturing they need as they begin to work out their new identity through Jesus.

Testimony

Larry was as rough and hard-nosed as they come. He had red hair that would light up a room and a fiery personality to go with it. He managed strip clubs, was addicted to drugs, drove a Harley, and couldn't say a sentence without vulgar language spewing out of his mouth. Larry's parents lived across the street from a young World Impact missionary who was pastoring a local church. Larry would come visit his parents and since he and the missionary were near the same age, they struck up a friendship. At first, Larry would do all he could to show off his wild and dangerous lifestyle and make sure that the young pastor knew nothing would change. But, the little church began to pray for Larry and the Spirit began to soften his heart.

Little by little, Larry showed up more, intrigued by this new and strange group of people in his former stomping grounds. He soon

A Strong and Courageous Church

began to ask lots of questions and before they knew it, Larry came to a point of brokenness and surrender to God. Immediately, he was fully embraced by the little urban church and soon got baptized and became a church member with roles and responsibilities. Larry played the bass on the worship team, read Scripture, gave testimony, and provided much of the muscle in moving the sound equipment in and out of the church's temporary location each week. Larry had tattoos all over him but the ones that stuck out the most were nearly naked ladies on his arms. When Larry got a break from playing bass, he would stand on the front row and raise his arms high in the air and everyone had to look past his tattoos as they faced the screen up front. Even though the church leaders lovingly encouraged Larry to wear long sleeve shirts, honestly, it did not matter that much because everyone was so overjoyed to see the transformation that had taken place in his life. Their church had a new family member and he knew he belonged!

COUNTING THE COST OVERVIEW

Clear Goals

- Welcome and Incorporation
- Orientation
- Preparing for Baptism
- Charting the Course of Discipleship

Critical Concepts and Perspectives

- The Church as the Family of God
- The Ways of the Family
- The Vulnerability of the Young
- The Radical Call of Christ

Crucial Checkpoints and Processes

- A Revolutionary Vision
- A Disciplined Walk
- A Believing Stance
- Process

Core Tools

- *Fight the Good Fight of Faith*
- *Book of Shared Spirituality*
- Community Resources

Clear Goals

§1 COUNTING THE COST

Discipleship should have clear goals during each stage of growth. Having clear goals will help you prioritize and form their interactions with those you are leading in discipleship.

The Clear Goals in this stage of discipleship are:

1. Welcome and Incorporation
2. Orientation
3. Preparing for Baptism
4. Charting the Course of Discipleship

1. Welcome and Incorporation

The top priority in the earliest stage of discipleship is warmly inviting people into your shared life. We should not set up barriers for our welcome of new people. Before lives will change, and very often before saving faith is reached, they will have to experience the family of God.

Be the Church

The best welcome and incorporation plan you can make is to craft the kind of community that warmly welcomes outsiders. While you need a plan in mind, welcome is less about the steps you take in your welcome program and more about the richness of life and fellowship in your community. Your ability to welcome and incorporate people depends entirely on your shared life right now.

2. Orientation

Assume Nothing! Hide Nothing!

Never assume that new Christians know even the basics of the Bible, how or why we pray, or what is going to happen in a church service. Don't assume they will automatically understand why things like coming to church, reading their Bible, or praying are important.

No one likes a 'bait and switch.' Do your best to be clear about what is going to happen, what is expected of them, and what it means to be a part of the church.

Make People Comfortable

Alleviate the awkwardness of being unfamiliar. Sometimes people are put off simply because they don't know what to do, and they feel awkward, out of place, and alone.

Provide the immediate care they need as brand new Christians.

When the Lord gives you the honor of seeing someone won to Christ, a brand new baby born in the faith, he also gives you the responsibility to care for them. Infants need attention and nurture to mature.

- Follow up with people as soon as possible. Don't let days and weeks pass before you visit or contact them.

- Get them a copy of the Bible and help them learn to navigate it by teaching them about the Testaments, books, and the chapter and verse structure.

- Make sure someone is staying in regular contact with them.

3. Preparing Them for a Beautiful and Powerful Baptism

Baptism has the potential to be one of the most significant moments in someone's life. It can be a lifetime 'fork in the road' that serves as the foundation for the rest of their baptized life in Christ. We need to prepare new believers for this momentous occasion.

The Significance of Baptism – *Birth and Citizenship in the New Creation*

- Baptism is obedience to both the example and the command of Christ (Matt 28.19). We follow him as king and Lord!

- Baptism is the union with Christ in his death, burial and resurrection (Rom 6.3–5). We have his eternal life!

- Baptism is our union with the body of Christ, the church, and a pledge to live as a representative of Christ in the world (Titus 2.14). We are citizens of his kingdom!

- Don't ever let baptism become cheap, small, or mundane in your fellowship. Baptism should be one of happiest, most celebratory things we do as the church!

The Act of Baptism – *Pledging Allegiance to the Kingdom of God*

When people transfer their citizenship from one nation to another, they must renounce their former allegiances, and pledge allegiance to their new country. We pledge allegiance to the kingdom of God and the Lord Jesus Christ by renouncing [rejecting] the dominion of darkness and making vows to Christ with the rest of his people.

This movement from the dominion of darkness to the Kingdom of the Son shapes the heart of CTV's Liturgy of Baptism. As you see below, we first reject the devil, the world, and the flesh, and turn to Jesus as Lord. Then we make our vows to Christ and his kingdom.

> **Rejection of the Devil, the World, and the Flesh (cutting off citizenship in the kingdom of darkness)**
>
> Question: Do you renounce Satan, the dominion of darkness, and all the spiritual forces of evil that rebel and war against God? If so, respond 'I renounce them.'
>
> Answer: I renounce them.
>
> Question: Do you renounce the evil powers of this world which corrupt and destroy the creatures of God? If so, respond 'I renounce them.'
>
> Answer: I renounce them.
>
> Question: Do you renounce all the sinful desires of your flesh that entice you away from loving and obeying God? If so, respond 'I renounce them.'
>
> Answer: I renounce them.
>
> Question: Do you trust Jesus Christ as your Savior, put your faith completely in him, and promise to obey his commands? If so, respond 'Jesus is Lord.'
> Answer: Jesus is Lord.

Making Vows to Christ with the Church: Together we all affirm...

Question: Do you join with the church in believing and affirming the scriptural witness to the person and work of God the Father, the Son, and the Holy Spirit, summarized by the Creed, and will you remain faithful to the teachings of the apostles and the prophets? If so, respond 'I believe the Truth.'

Answer: I believe the Truth.

Question: Will you share with the church in worshipping the true and living God, as a member of the royal priesthood, and will you live always for the glory of God alone? If so, respond 'I will worship the King.'

Answer: I will worship the King.

Question: Will you daily take up your cross with the church and follow the Lord Jesus, being conformed to his image by the Holy Spirit, resisting sin and evil, and disciplining yourself for godliness by the grace that God supplies? If so, respond 'I will follow Jesus, the Nazarene.'

Answer: I will follow Jesus, the Nazarene.

Question: Will you enlist with the church and put on the full armor of God so that you may carry out the mission of Jesus to advance God's kingdom in the world and to destroy the works of the devil? If so, respond 'I will serve the Lord.'

Answer: I will serve the Lord.

4. Charting the Course of Discipleship

In everything, make clear that conversion to Christ is conversion to a life of discipleship. They will continue to reject the world, the flesh, and the devil, affirm Jesus as Lord and live in his kingdom every day from now on.

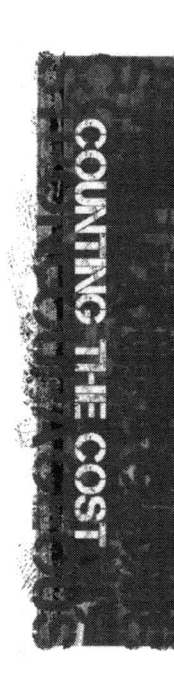

COUNTING THE COST

A Strong and Courageous Church

We tend to speak of salvation as what happened at the beginning of our walk with Christ. While it is fine to place emphasis on the initial decision to follow Christ, we must be equally as concerned that people make the decision to keep following Christ when it gets difficult and dark. Salvation is not simply making a beginning with Jesus, it is picking up our cross daily, and suffering with him in order that we may be glorifies with him (Luke 9.23; Rom 8.17).

Help them count the cost of a life in Christ!

Critical Concepts and Perspectives

§1 COUNTING THE COST

The critical concepts and perspectives we must have in each stage of discipleship will help you view your discipleship process through the lens of what is most important for a new believer to learn and grow in.

The Clear Concepts and Perspectives We Must Have in this stage of discipleship are:

CONCEPTS
1. The Church as God's Family
2. The Ways of the Family

PERSPECTIVES
1. The Radical Call of Christ
2. The Vulnerability of the Young

CONCEPTS

During the early stages of discipleship it is important to remember that the church is God's family and we must quickly and joyfully embrace and incorporate new believers into this family.

1. The Church as God's Family

The Family of God is a rich biblical image of nurture, support, love, and connection that is especially helpful as we consider early discipleship. God chose this imagery because of the strong connection between our experience in the human family and our experience as a spiritual family. It is hard to overestimate the importance of the church as a family for a young believer. The realities of immaturity, vulnerability, and unfamiliarity are all addressed through our life as a family.

Biblical Images of Salvation and the Church

- **New Birth/Regeneration (John 3.3–8; Titus 3.5)** – We are born anew as God's own children. The imagery of birth pictures entry into a family.

- **Adoption (Galatians 4.4–7)** – Though we are not children by nature, he has chosen us for himself, and given us an inheritance. Again, adoption pictures entry into a family.

- **The Household of God (1 Timothy 3.15; Romans 8.12–17)** – The church is the family of God's children, a household under Jesus our Lord. In him, we are bound together more firmly than even natural families.

This imagery has profound implications for our understanding and practice of discipleship. Young believers are meant to discover who they are in Christ and what it means to follow him through the life of the family.

The Young Need a Family

The best thing we can do is to nurture them like a family nurtures a new arrival. Research has shown time and time again that a poor family structure has a destructive and lasting effect on children. No matter how things appear, a new believer is not spiritually self-sufficient and they should not be left to fend for themselves without a family.

One of the most damaging things we can communicate to a new believer is that Christianity is basically an individual matter. *However, this is exactly what they learn when we make discipleship entirely a matter of personal responsibility.* New believers must be fully embraced into the shared life and spirituality of your church.

The Young Need to be Taught the Ways of the Family.

Be Clear – It is easy to under-explain things to the young by making assumptions about very basic understanding. It is also easy to over-explain things to the young by leading them into debates and controversies before they have the solid truth. The focus in early discipleship must be to ground new believers in the core truths of the faith.

Be Concrete – Use simple and tangible means to teach complex and intangible truth. When children learn to walk, they do not first need to know the biology of knee ligaments or the physics of gravity and force. They don't need to know grammar or the historical development of language to say "Mama…Dada." They learn to speak and walk by the tangible and visible example of their parents.

In the same fashion, we as the church need to leverage the tangible and visible ways of our family for discipleship. Of course we want believers to love God with all their heart, soul, mind, and strength, and to love their neighbors as themselves. For the young in faith, however, we must be able to give them clear concrete expressions of that love in these different areas of life.

2. The Ways of the Family

As Christ the Victor churches, we identify with four specific ways in which we respond to God's saving acts and live out our new identities in Christ. *Each of these responses has **tangible and visible** expressions in our church life that we can use for discipleship.*

We Believe the Truth

We are reborn into a new world where things may look the same, but where everything is different! We need to provide new believers with an introduction to this new world, teaching them what is true. However, we cannot start with big philosophical or abstract ideas. Start with the basic storyline of the Bible with Christ as it main theme and hero. We use the clear concrete statement of the Nicene Creed as a summary of the Bible.

We Worship the King

Part of the Christian life is reorienting our hearts (what we love and what we want) toward the Lord and his kingdom. We can help the young begin this journey by explaining the tangible and visible expression of our adoration in the liturgy, not just in its mechanics, but in its spiritual content and meaning.

We Follow the Nazarene

In our Christian journey, the Holy Spirit remakes us in the image of Jesus. We can teach the young how to walk this journey by the clear, concrete spiritual disciplines of the BOSS (*Book of Shared Spirituality*). There are daily Bible readings, memory verses, prayers, and devotions. We can use the Lord's Prayer to teach people how to pray. We can use the Ten Commandments to teach ethics (see Appx 8, p.109). [But don't let people get the wrong idea as if these earn Christ-likeness. Teach these as means of grace, that is the avenues by which the Lord will pour out transforming and empowering grace into their lives.]

We Serve the Lord

The Christian life is a life of service and mission. We have a new purpose in

Christ's kingdom and calling to reach everyone with the gospel.

We start the young on this path by teaching them to talk about their testimony and to give a simple gospel presentation. Teach them to love and serve others by incorporating them into existing ministries of the church. Make intentional places where baby Christians can serve without endangering themselves or others.

PERSPECTIVES WE MUST HAVE

During the early stages of discipleship it is important to keep in mind the radical call of Christ and how vulnerable new believers are. They need to be both challenged and cared for.

1. The Radical Call of Christ (Luke 9.57–62)

Don't lowball the cost of following Christ. There will be costs for young urban disciples: personal, psychological, familial, and social. Don't soften the call in order to make it easier. It is very easy to get into sales-person mode talking up the benefits and downplaying difficulties. Failing to acknowledge the radical nature of Christ's call is a recipe for having young disciples go back to their former lives.

2. The Vulnerability of the Young (2 Pet. 2.18–22)

The enemy is described as a prowling lion, looking for someone to devour. Lions do not hunt the strong and mature, they live on the weak, the sick, and the young who are too slow to get away. New believers are not yet trained and outfitted to deflect the outright assaults of the devil. Their senses are not yet trained to detect the subtle attacks of the evil one. You will need to help them identify areas of weakness and give them tools to protect themselves.

This is especially pronounced in urban poor environments where there are very often significant entanglements to be undone such as addiction, family dysfunction, gang affiliations, and generational poverty cycles. Your church needs to be ready to stand in the gap for these new family members, being a true family to those who may have left the only support structures they have known as they follow Christ. You will need to arm yourself with resources that address these needs and connections in your community that can give vital support to new believers. Walk with them in this process so that they do not feel alone.

Crucial Checkpoints and Processes

§1 COUNTING THE COST

At each stage of discipleship you should have clear checkpoints to use as benchmarks of growth and there should be specific steps worked into your discipleship plans.

The Crucial Checkpoints and Processes in this stage of discipleship are:

CHECKPOINTS

1. A Revolutionary Vision
2. A Disciplined Walk
3. A Believing Stance

PROCESSES

1. Be a Friend and a Family
2. Ensure Understanding of the Gospel and of Salvation.
3. Prepare for Baptism.
4. Teach Basic Spiritual Disciplines.
5. Make Immediate Opportunities for Ministry.

CHECKPOINTS

In the early stage of discipleship it can be difficult to determine what areas of growth are most important. Here are a few checkpoints to look for in a growing disciple. Taken from *Fit to Represent* (see appendix 2, p. 89).

1. A Revolutionary Vision

Viewing Everything through the Story of God (1 Corinthians 2.9–16)

One true sign of growth is a new believer's ability to recognize their place in the Story of God. You should begin to see the following things in a growing believer's view of themselves and the world:

- Solid conversion in Christ through faith and repentance
- Christ and his kingdom relating to every area of life
- Connection to the body of Christ, the church, as new family
- Taking on the yoke of Christ and humbly learning from him

2. A Disciplined Walk

Spiritual Formation (1 Timothy 4.7–16)

A disciplined walk will not be automatic in a new believer's life. It will take time for them to practice their faith consistently. To know there is legitimate growth occurring, look for the following things in their lives:

- Keeping in step with the Holy Spirit
- Communion with God
- Ingestion of the Word

- Prayer and Worship

- Personal Holiness

- Submission to pastoral leadership and community life

3. A Believing Stance

Defending the Apostolic Faith (Colossians 2.6–10)

A new believer should take ownership of their faith. You should begin to see them handling the core truths of God's Word with real understanding. They should evidence the following things in their lives:

- Hunger for God's Word (teachable)

- Grounded in an understanding of the Nicene Creed and the gospel of Christ

- Grasping and telling the Kingdom story – Creation: Incarnation: New Creation

PROCESSES

During the early stage of discipleship you are responsible for leading a new believer through key steps in their spiritual growth. This checklist can serve as a process of key steps to include in your discipleship plan.

- ☑ Be a friend and a family

- ☑ Ensure understanding of the gospel and of salvation.

- ☑ Prepare for baptism.

- ☑ Teach basic spiritual disciplines.
  - ✓ Disciplines of the Word – Reading, memorization, meditation
  - ✓ Prayer
  - ✓ Worship
  - ✓ Fellowship

- ☑ Make immediate opportunities for ministry.
  - ✓ In the Church – Giving testimony, contributing to the life of the church
  - ✓ Outside the Church – Evangelism, service

Core Tools

§1 COUNTING THE COST

At each stage of discipleship you should have go-to resources that will help you guide believers toward maturity.

Some Core Tools in this stage of discipleship are:

1. Fight the Good Fight of Faith
2. Book of Shared Spirituality
3. Community Resources

1. Fight the Good Fight of Faith

Fight the Good Fight of Faith is a practical, helpful resource especially designed to help new and growing Christians become effective disciples/warriors of Christ, and is built entirely on the Story of God as told in the Scriptures. It can also serve as an official precursor to TUMI's Capstone Curriculum seminary training, providing a solid introduction to the Bible's major themes as well as the foundational principles of Christian discipleship. *Fight the Good Fight of Faith can be purchased on Amazon.*

2. Book of Shared Spirituality

The *Christ the Victor Book of Shared Spirituality* (BOSS) serves as a guide to experiencing Christ's victory in our churches and lives through a Christ-centered shared spirituality. It guides your corporate worship gatherings, and provides a framework to walk through the church year together, even as you practice spiritual disciplines alone. For example, you may meet in small groups or in a discipleship setting throughout the week to further discuss the weekly lectionary texts, and encourage one another to engage in the daily reading routine and scripture memorization provided in the BOSS. *The BOSS can be purchased on Amazon.*

3. Community Resources

Your church may want to compile a list of community resources that will help address some of the particular needs of new urban believers. You will want to begin to develop relationships with key contacts and ministries so that you can quickly refer your church members for the specialized care and support they need. This may include knowing of local drug and alcohol rehabilitation programs, financially accessible Christian counselling centers, shelters for families in transition or for battered women and children, employment opportunities, and educational programs for adult education.

§2

OVER THE HUMP

Equipping the Saints for the Work of the Ministry

Joshua at Kadesh Barnea (Numbers 14) – *Standing Among the Leaders*

Joshua is at the center of the one of the greatest tragedies in the history of Israel, the rebellion at Kadesh-Barnea. After the twelve spy out the land, the reports of a giant warrior people dishearten Israel so that they try to choose a new leader who will take them back to Egypt. Numbers 14.6–8 says, "And Joshua the son of Nun and Caleb the son of Jephunneh, who were among those who had spied out the land, tore their clothes 7 and said to all the congregation of the people of Israel, 'The land, which we passed through to spy it out, is an exceedingly good land. 8 If the LORD delights in us, he will bring us into this land and give it to us, a land that flows with milk and honey.'"

Joshua and Caleb stand with Moses in opposition to their peers. Moses is still in charge, but these guys are bearing the burden here of the people's rebellion. Joshua has moved over the hump from devoted apprentice to active participant in leadership with Moses.

Over the Hump

Just as Joshua and Caleb became active participants in leading the Israelites through their witness, maturing believers should begin to join with their leaders in service. There should come a time in the life of a disciple when they are no longer teetering on the brink falling back, but are clearly established in the Lord. Our hope in discipleship is to help people grow to the point where they take ownership of their own faith and spiritual life and become co-laborers in the work of ministry.

> [11] *About this we have much to say, and it is hard to explain, since you have become dull of hearing.* [12] *For though* **by this time you ought to be teachers***, you need someone to teach you again the basic principles of the oracles of God. You need milk, not solid food,* [13] *for everyone who lives on milk is unskilled in the word of righteousness, since he is a child.* [14] *But* **solid food is for the mature***, for those who have their powers of discernment trained by constant practice to distinguish good from evil.* [6.1] *Therefore let us leave the elementary doctrine of Christ and* **go on to maturity***, not laying again a foundation of repentance from dead works and of faith toward God,* [2] *and of instruction about washings, the laying on of hands, the resurrection of the dead, and eternal judgment.* [3] *And this we will do if God permits.* Hebrews 5.11–6.3 (ESV)

For a believer to make it "Over the Hump," moving steadily toward being a "Mature Christian," you will need to provide consistent support and challenge, as well as the work of equipping them to serve the Lord in the ways they are gifted and called to serve (as illustrated in the chart below).

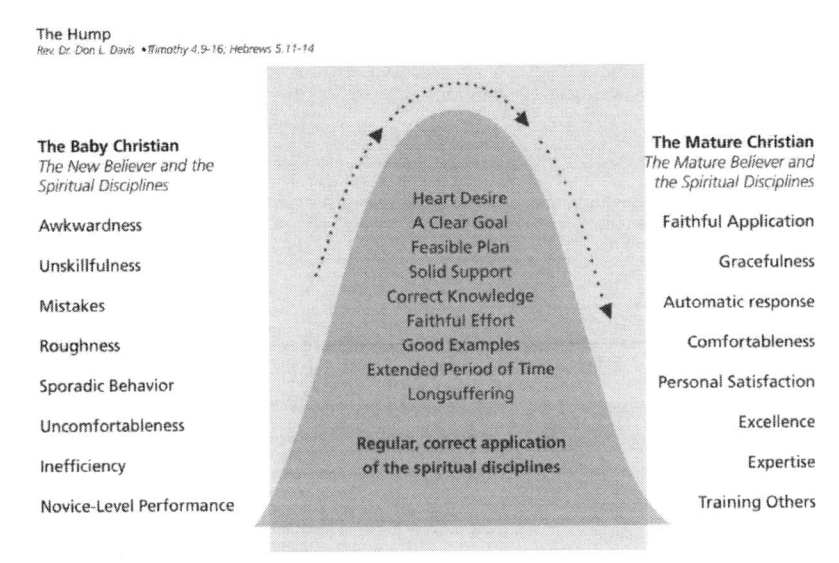

The Hump
Rev. Dr. Don L. Davis • *1Timothy 4.9-16; Hebrews 5.11-14*

The Baby Christian *The New Believer and the Spiritual Disciplines*		The Mature Christian *The Mature Believer and the Spiritual Disciplines*
Awkwardness	Heart Desire A Clear Goal	Faithful Application
Unskillfulness	Feasible Plan Solid Support	Gracefulness
Mistakes	Correct Knowledge Faithful Effort	Automatic response
Roughness	Good Examples	Comfortableness
Sporadic Behavior	Extended Period of Time Longsuffering	Personal Satisfaction
Uncomfortableness		Excellence
Inefficiency	Regular, correct application of the spiritual disciplines	Expertise
Novice-Level Performance		Training Others

© 2004. The Urban Ministry Institute. All Rights Reserved. The Urban Ministry Institute is a ministry of World Impact, Inc.

What Does This Look Like?

The Church is God's Temple

As a believer matures and embraces their place in the family of God, they should also begin to understand the church as God's temple. The church is where God's kingdom is represented in the world. A maturing believer grows to demonstrate the life of the kingdom individually and corporately. They need to be encouraged to live through the power of the Holy Spirit as a member of the royal priesthood of God.

At this stage in a believer's growth they should have roles to play in the rhythms of the church. They should begin to understand what spiritual gifts they have and how they can be used to edify the church. The faithfulness with which they use these gifts will determine their continued growth.

Testimony

We don't use the word temple much anymore and appropriately so as we call the visible body of Christ, the church. However, the idea of believers being priests in God's Temple is a powerful image that we need to reclaim today.

The first Christ the Victor Church started with humble beginnings in a missionary's basement. As the church grew, they moved to another missionary house that could hold 40-50 people. As CTV was still forming in identity and practice, one of the things the leadership wanted was to emphasize and perhaps even experiment a bit with, this idea of the priesthood of all believers. So a plan was set into action and the leadership team developed a chart of responsibilities for members and faithful attenders. They rotated everything in the sacred service from the opening and welcome, to lighting the candles, to reading Scripture, preaching, prayer, and communion. It was a good system where people tried out new areas and sometimes it fell flat but more times than not, it startled people and led to thoughts like, "I didn't

A Strong and Courageous Church

know they could do that!"

Through prayer and feedback, each participant grew in the areas they had gifting. Over and over the congregation talked about how much they enjoyed hearing a different preacher each week. While this may not be the model for every church setting, it certainly revealed the power of getting people involved, not just in the work of ministry outside the church to a hurting world, but also inside the church, ministering to one another through the weekly sacred service.

It was by no means perfect in those early days and the church had its share of trials managing a lot of young and growing Christians serving in a variety of roles, but the members experienced the body of Christ ministering to each other and it was a little bit of heaven!

OVER THE HUMP OVERVIEW

Clear Goals

- Stability in Christ and in the Church
- Commitment to Christ and His Kingdom
- The 2 Timothy 2.2 Progression
- Discovering, Developing, and Using Gifts with Excellence

Critical Concepts and Perspectives

- The Church as God's Temple
- Living the Victory
- Seeking the Advance of His Kingdom
- Standing on the Ancient Faith
- Only Disciples Make Disciples
- Becoming Actors in the Drama
- A Warrior Mentality

Crucial Checkpoints and Processes

- A Shared Life in Common
- A Fighting Spirit
- Process

Core Tools

- *Fight the Good Fight of Faith*
- *Book of Shared Spirituality*
- *CTV Raising the Banner High*
- SIAFU Resources and Retreats
- TUMI Foundations Courses

OVER THE HUMP

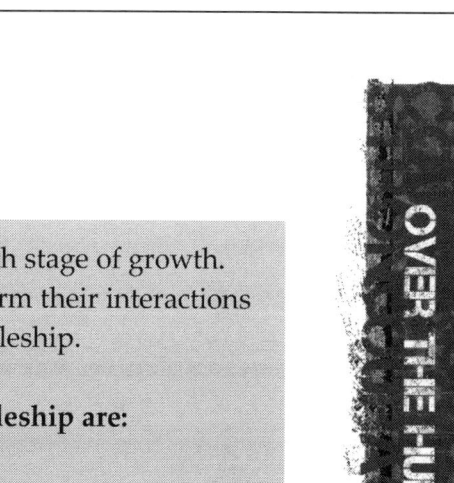

Clear Goals
§2 OVER THE HUMP

Discipleship should have clear goals during each stage of growth. Having clear goals will help you prioritize and form their interactions with those you are leading in discipleship.

The Clear Goals in this stage of discipleship are:

1. **Stability in Christ and in the Church**
2. **Commitment to Christ and His Kingdom**
3. **The 2 Timothy 2.2 Progression**
4. **Discovering, Developing, and Using Gifts with Excellence**

1. Stability in Christ and in the Church

We want to see people established as a part of the maturing body (Ephesians 4.13–16). Their lives should increasingly represent Christ and his Church. This doesn't mean that they will not make mistakes or need consistent shepherding, but our goal in discipleship is to see a believer grow more stable in living out their life in Christ.

2. Internal Commitment and Allegiance to Christ and His Kingdom

We want to inspire a direct allegiance to Christ and his kingdom rather than simply an allegiance to a certain church or leader. It is important for a disciple to submit to the local leadership of their church, and to learn to represent their church body, but only in the context of their allegiance to Christ and the advancing of his Kingdom. A maturing believer should feel compelled to engage in meaningful Kingdom work with like-minded believers.

3. The 2 Timothy 2.2 Progression

2 Timothy 2.2 says "…what you have heard from me in the presence of many witnesses entrust to faithful men who will be able to teach others also." (ESV). Our goals in discipleship should follow this progression:

- Identify receptive and teachable disciples.

- Train the faithful, and entrust them with responsibility and authority.

- Release them to reproduce.

4. Discovering, Developing, and Using Gifts with Excellence

Discovering Gifts

Find opportunities for people to explore their giftedness. This may take some trial and error. Listen to what they are passionate about and take note of the areas they are quick to offer their service. Begin to give growing believers small areas of leadership and debrief together on the results. Some people's gifts are immediately obvious, but other people need attentive guidance as they begin to discover how the Spirit has gifted them for service. No matter how hidden or apparent, each gift is necessary for the building up of the church and discovering what gifts are among you should be given great priority.

Developing Gifts

Provide ongoing training, opportunity, and feedback as people use their gifts. Identifying people's gifts is only the beginning of the process. You must then provide them with significant ways to serve and lead in areas that utilize their gifts. They will always need someone to walk intentionally with them in the process, giving them training to apply their gifts and constructive criticism as they go. This may look like someone with the gift of service shadowing a mature believer who already serves well or having someone with the gift of teaching assist a well-seasoned teacher in a Bible study class.

Using Gifts with Excellence

Help people come into full bloom in the use of their gifts, and don't let yourself feel threatened by their excellence. Release people to really lead! It is important to expect continued growth and excellence in areas you have given people authority, but don't be heavy-handed. Empower them to serve and to expand God's Kingdom in the way that he leads them.

OVER THE HUMP

Critical Concepts and Perspectives

§2 OVER THE HUMP

The critical concepts and perspectives we must have in each stage of discipleship will help you view your discipleship process through the lens of what is most important for a new believer to learn and grow in.

The Clear Concepts and Perspectives We Must Have in this stage of discipleship are:

CONCEPTS

1. The Church as God's Temple
2. Living the Victory
3. Seeking the Advance of His Kingdom
4. Standing on the Ancient Faith

PERSPECTIVES

1. Only Disciples Make Disciples
2. Becoming Actors in the Drama
3. A Warrior Mentality

CONCEPTS

As discipleship begins to focus on maturing a believer it is important to envision the Church as God's temple, where an emerging leader lives out victory in Christ, seeks the advance of his kingdom, and is grounded in the ancient faith.

1. The Church as God's Temple (1 Corinthians 3.16)

A growing believer must embrace the image of the Church as God's temple. They must be taught what it means to be a priest in God's temple and that they are anointed and gifted by God for his service.

Biblical Images of Salvation and the Church

This imagery has profound implications for our understanding of discipleship. A disciple needs to be instructed in how to live out the truth that they are:

- **The Temple of the Holy Spirit** (Ephesians 2.20–22) – We are a dwelling place for God by his Spirit. Through Christ, we have access by faith to most intimate fellowship with the Almighty himself. As his temple, his presence in the world flows uniquely through the church.

- **A Royal Priesthood** (1 Peter 2.9) – Everyone of us is ordained for service before the Lord. *Every believer* is anointed, gifted, and called to worship and serve God. Just as the priests were cleansed with water, clothed in new garments, purified with blood, and anointed with oil, so too we are washed in baptism, clothed in Christ's righteousness, purified by his blood, and anointed with the Spirit.

- **A Living Sacrifice** (Romans 12.1–2) – As priests, the sacrifice we offer is ourselves! We put our very lives on the altar as a living sacrifice that honors him.

The Implications of this Imagery

We are the arena (locus) of God's kingdom in the world today, the place where God's redemption and presence can be seen and touched. Every one of us, from the newest to the oldest in Christ is anointed, gifted, and called for the work of ministry.

There is a priestly rhythm that is woven into the fabric of what it means to be the people of God.

- The priests had daily, weekly, monthly, seasonal, and yearly schedules of worship, sacrifices, festivals, and fasts that formed the rhythm of their life.

- As priests of the Lord, the church also partakes of these rhythms in daily times with Lord, weekly worship, and seasonal or yearly celebrations and fasts through the church year.

- There was also a dynamic interplay between the communal, familial, and individual spheres in their worship. Some celebrations involved the entire nation, some were carried out by each household, and some of the worship was very personal and individual.

- As the church, we also experience in our shared spirituality the dynamic interplay of communal worship, family or smaller group practices, and individual devotion.

2. Living the Victory (1 John 3.7–8)

The world, the flesh, and the devil are being overcome! The life of the kingdom manifest is one where the works of the devil are destroyed. As Christ the Victor churches, we are committed to living out this victory in our own lives, in our churches, and in our communities. A life truly submitted to Christ must show evidence of his victory at every level. The

restoration of Christ is all encompassing, shining light into every dark corner of our lives, delivering us from all manner of sin and evil.

3. Seeking the Advance of His Kingdom (Acts 1.8)

New Purpose and Vision – The Great Commission

The Great Commission of Christ points our lives in a new direction. Your church should build into disciples a strong and contagious vision for your "Jerusalem," "Judea," and "Samaria" and even "the ends of the earth!"

Full Participation as an Agent of the Kingdom

The local church and the individual believer within that congregation are full participants in the Great Commission. It should be in the heart of each person to see the victory of Christ win those who are in bondage to the enemy. As disciples mature, they should begin to embrace the Great Commission as a personal mandate. We should equip people to honestly say, 'I can be a part of this great story.' This will give your church dynamic ways to reach your community through the unique gifting of your members.

4. Standing on the Ancient Faith (Jude 3)

Key to our Christian foundation is the tradition passed down to us through the church. Each local body will have unique expressions of these core truths but a growing believer should be able to understand and teach others in, as Vincent of Lerins in AD 434 declared, "that which has been believed everywhere, always and by all." Your disciples should evidence solid:

- Articulation – They are able to tell what we believe

- Explanation and Defense – They are able to expound and defend our beliefs with Scripture

- Reproduction – They are able to teach what we believe to someone else

PERSPECTIVES WE MUST HAVE

As discipleship begins to focus on maturing a believer, it is important to keep in mind that only disciples make disciples and emerging leaders need to embrace a warrior's mentality to advance God's kingdom.

1. Only Disciples Make Disciples

At its heart discipleship can never be reduced to a curriculum or method-based system. It is always a matter of mature godly people investing in and training up the young until we all reach maturity together. At each stage of growth there is opportunity to draw others on toward Christ. As a leader, you also need to intentionally seek continued spiritual growth because only disciples can make disciples.

2. Becoming Actors in the Drama

Disciples must learn to become actors in the story of God rather than merely being acted upon. We want to see people fully owning their identity and role in God's story. They must learn to view themselves not as a receptacle of grace, but as a conduit of grace for their world. True growth in ministry comes when believers are able to turn their focus outward and begin to participate in what God is doing in lives around them.

3. A Warrior Mentality

Disciples must learn to engage in the spiritual battle through experienced use of the armor of the Lord. We do not war against flesh and blood with weapons of destruction! We wage war against the powers of evil and darkness with spiritual weapons of love, truth, prayer, righteousness, and salvation through the gospel.

A Warrior is Disciplined and Ready

It is important for us to understand that the Lord has outfitted us for battle, and he expects us to engage in warfare. We take hold of the armor that the Lord provides knowing that the battle belongs to him! We do not have to walk in fear because there is no power of darkness that can stand against Christ.

A Warrior is Aware and Alert

We are not ignorant of our enemy or his schemes. We must constantly remember that we are in a war, and that our enemy does not fight fair. Vigilance is key to engaging in spiritual warfare and people must be watchful at all times.

Crucial Checkpoints and Processes

§2 OVER THE HUMP

At each stage of discipleship you should have clear checkpoints to use as benchmarks of growth and there should be specific steps worked into your discipleship plans.

The Crucial Checkpoints and Processes in this stage of discipleship are:

CHECKPOINTS
1. A Shared Life in Common
2. A Fighting Spirit

PROCESSES
1. Formation of Church Life
2. Demonstrations of Maturity
3. Communication through Methods

CHECKPOINTS

As believers mature here are a few checkpoints to look for in an emerging leader. Taken from *Fit to Represent* (see appendix 2, p. 89).

☑☑ 1. A Shared Life in Common: Church, Marriage, Family (Acts 2.42–47)

A true sign that a believer is getting over the hump is when they begin to evidence consistent and apparent Christ-likeness in community and relationship. You should see the following things becoming realities in their lives:

- Strong incorporation and participation in the life of the local church
- Marriage and family relationship being redeemed
- Discovery and use of the gifts

☑☑ 2. A Fighting Spirit: Spiritual Warfare (Ephesians 6.10–18)

A maturing believer has a fighting spirit, demonstrated by putting on the whole armor of God. Someone who is ready and willing to engage in the spiritual warfare must have these key attributes:

- Awareness of the lies and schemes of the enemy
- Identity as a soldier of Christ
- Disciplined commitment to the Word and prayer as the weapons of warfare
- Walking in the power of the Spirit
- Armed with the mind to suffer for Christ

PROCESS

As you identify and train emerging leaders this checklist can serve as a process of key steps to include in your discipleship plan.

The life of Christ forms the life of the church, is demonstrated in the lives of mature disciples, and is communicated through services, teachings, classes, groups, and mentoring relationships in the church.

- ☑ Be Intentional About the Formation of Church Life
    - ✓ The church year sets that context and path for our discipleship journey.
    - ✓ Christ's own life provides the spiritual content of our life together. It emphasizes the various phases of Christ's story as his life formed in us.
    - ✓ We experience his presence and life in our midst as we follow him together.

- ☑ Look for Demonstrations of Maturity
    - ✓ The more mature disciples help the young on the journey, caring for them, teaching them, and encouraging them.
    - ✓ By the presence and power of the Holy Spirit, we display the person of Jesus in our lives both individually and collectively.

- ☑ Embrace the Freedom of Communication through Methods
    - ✓ Everything is as at our disposal. We are not married to any particular tool or methodology.
    - ✓ The services, teachings, classes, groups, and mentoring relationships in the church are the tools for discipleship, not discipleship itself.

OVER THE HUMP

Core Tools
§2 OVER THE HUMP

At each stage of discipleship you should have go-to resources that will help you guide believers toward maturity.

Some Core Tools in this stage of discipleship are:

1. Fight the Good Fight of Faith
2. Book of Shared Spirituality
3. CTV Raising the Banner High
4. SIAFU Resources and Retreats
5. TUMI Foundations Courses

1. Fight the Good Fight of Faith

Fight the Good Fight of Faith is a practical, helpful resource especially designed to help new and growing Christians become effective disciples/warriors of Christ, and is built entirely on the Story of God as told in the Scriptures. It can also serve as an official precursor to TUMI's Capstone Curriculum seminary training, providing a solid introduction to the Bible's major themes as well as the foundational principles of Christian discipleship. *Fight the Good Fight of Faith can be purchased on Amazon.*

2. Book of Shared Spirituality

The *Christ the Victor Book of Shared Spirituality* (BOSS) serves as a guide to experiencing Christ's victory in our churches and lives through a Christ-centered shared spirituality. It guides your corporate worship gatherings, and provides a framework to walk through the church year together, even as you practice spiritual disciplines alone. For example, you may begin to let your disciples lead areas of the worship service, or assist in leading small groups. The framework provided in the BOSS allows for clear expectations and provides the important information that will guide them as they lead. *The BOSS can be purchased on Amazon.*

3. CTV Raising the Banner High

Raising the Banner High: An Introduction to CTV, along with the companion DVD, is a training resource that explains the powerful common identity and rich shared practices of the Christ the Victor Churches. This is an important tool to ground your emerging leaders in the identity and practices of CTV. *Raising the Banner High can be purchased on Amazon.*

4. SIAFU Resources and Retreats

The SIAFU Network is a national association of chapters anchored in local urban churches and ministries dedicated to the city. SIAFU chapters are designed to help identify, equip and release spiritually qualified servant leaders to reach and transform our neediest, unreached communities in urban America. Named after the siafu (driver) ant of Africa, SIAFU operates on the understanding that alone we may be weak and vulnerable, but when we join together an army of "ants" can become an unstoppable movement. SIAFU retreats, offered regionally, are a great way to encourage and empower believers to advance God's Kingdom in their communities. *More information about SIAFU can be found at www.tumi.org.*

5. TUMI Foundations Courses

The Foundations for Ministry Series are resources of The Urban Ministry Institute (TUMI). The topics covered in these resources are foundational to effective urban ministry, and can be used by anyone seeking to equip leaders in urban churches. Topics include seminars such as *Winning the World, Vision for Mission, The Gospel of John, Church Matters, Marking Time*, and many others. *For more information on the tUMI Foundations Courses visit www.tumi.org.*

§3

FIT TO REPRESENT

The Next Generation of the Church

Joshua's Appointment by Moses (Deut. 31.1–8) – You will lead this people.

At the end of his life, Moses transfers authority and responsibility for Israel to Joshua. Deuteronomy 31.3 says, "The LORD your God himself will go over before you. He will destroy these nations before you, so that you shall dispossess them, and Joshua will go over at your head, as the LORD has spoken."

Joshua is the new Moses who will lead Israel into the promised land. He is in charge from here on in. Because of what has happened up to this point, he is able to step into this leadership with strength and courage!

Fit to Represent

A leader who is ready to be released for service has a clear call from God and has proven Christ-like character. They have also demonstrated an ability to walk by the power of the Holy Spirit and to care for the people of God. Just as with Timothy, they have proven worth in the service of the Lord.

> [19] *I hope in the Lord Jesus to send Timothy to you soon, so that I too may be cheered by news of you.* [20] *For* **I have no one like him, who will be genuinely concerned for your welfare.** [21] *For they all seek their own*

interests, not those of Jesus Christ. ²² *But you know Timothy's* **proven worth, how as a son with a father he has served with me in the gospel.** ²³ *I hope therefore to send him just as soon as I see how it will go with me,* ²⁴ *and I trust in the Lord that shortly I myself will come also.*
Philippians 2.19–24 (ESV)

Someone who is fit to represent Christ and his Church through leadership is a "Mature Christian" who not only serves with commitment and excellence, but who can graciously lead and train others (as illustrated in the following chart).

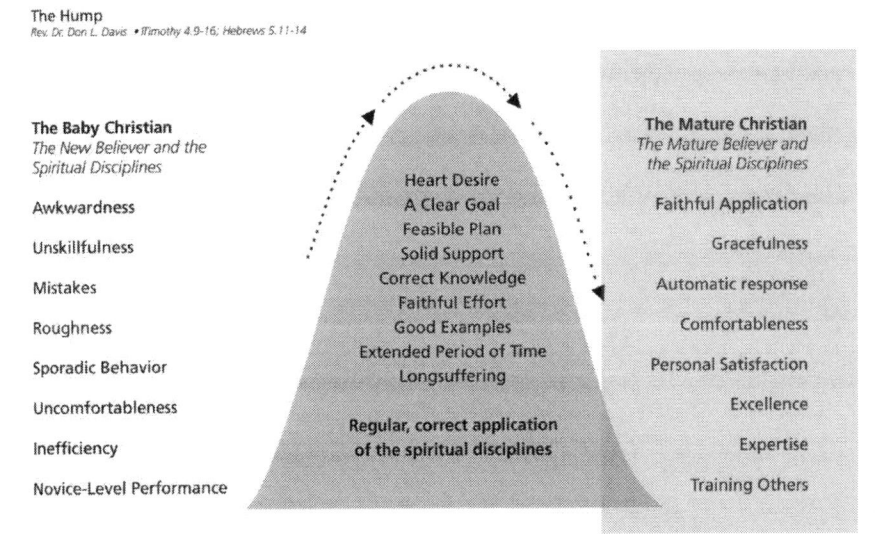

The Hump
Rev. Dr. Don L. Davis • 1Timothy 4.9-16; Hebrews 5.11-14

The Baby Christian *The New Believer and the Spiritual Disciplines*		The Mature Christian *The Mature Believer and the Spiritual Disciplines*
Awkwardness	Heart Desire	Faithful Application
Unskillfulness	A Clear Goal Feasible Plan Solid Support	Gracefulness
Mistakes	Correct Knowledge Faithful Effort	Automatic response
Roughness	Good Examples	Comfortableness
Sporadic Behavior	Extended Period of Time Longsuffering	Personal Satisfaction
Uncomfortableness		Excellence
Inefficiency	**Regular, correct application of the spiritual disciplines**	Expertise
Novice-Level Performance		Training Others

© 2004. The Urban Ministry Institute. All Rights Reserved. The Urban Ministry Institute is a ministry of World Impact, Inc.

What Does This Look Like?

The Church is God's Army

Mature believers identify as members of God's army. Someone who is ready to lead is a person who lives a disciplined walk and demonstrates mature gifts. They are able to live fully into their place in that army. Just as there are many ranks in the army, each will be called to lead in accordance with their gifts and calling, but each person is crucial to the advancement of God's kingdom.

An army also shares a unified vision and mission, with each member contributing towards and sacrificing for the completion of that mission. In the same way a mature believer's allegiance is to Christ and his kingdom, not to their own visions and ideas. They are able to serve others boldly, waging war against evil and darkness and declaring liberty to the captives!

Testimony

In 2016 two CTV churches were planted in two different units at Hutchinson Correctional Facility about an hour from Wichita. A class of The Urban Ministry Institute began in the maximum security unit three years prior and nine men committed themselves to taking and completing the Capstone Curriculum. Two of the students, Steve and Malachi were natural leaders and they often butt heads. The classes and to some extent the entire protestant "call-out" (a term used for the church services held inside the prison) were negatively impacted by their conflicts.

The situation worsened until they decided to ask men who had been discipling and training them, and who were also in CTV leadership, for help. Feeling a little out of place but armed with an approach based on Matthew 18, the CTV leaders engaged the situation. The Spirit of the Lord met them in a powerful way, bringing the conflict to a resolution and paving the way for these two men to grow into best friends. They even developed an agreement to begin growing in what it meant to participate in the life and ministry of CTV because they both had a call to start churches inside and outside the prison.

Intentional time in discipleship and training began with both Steve and Malachi, as they both began implementing CTV identity and practice at the protestant "call-out" which in turn helped it to grow as a more spiritually healthy church. But the Lord had even more plans for these two! They were soon moved to the medium security unity where there was a better opportunity to start a CTV "call-out" that would complement (not compete with!) the larger protestant "call-out." Eventually Steve was transferred to the minimum security unit where he was able to start a second CTV "call-out."

No one anticipated such rapid growth from these two men, but through their obvious commitment and intentional discipleship both Steve and

Malachi have become amazing and powerful leaders inside the walls of the prison, and are themselves training up other men to lead inside the prison and to be missionary pastors once released. When leadership development is taken seriously and disciplers refuse to compromise or lower our standards, God will prepare men and women for leadership in the CTV movement. May this only be the start!

FIT TO REPRESENT OVERVIEW

Clear Goals

- Discerning, Training, Authorizing, and Releasing Emerging Leaders
- Empowering the 'Variety of Gifts'
- Developing Disciples into the Next Generation of the Church

Critical Concepts and Perspectives

- The Church as God's Army
- Calling
- Character
- Competence
- Community
- The Sovereign Willing of the Spirit
- Leaders make Leaders
- High but Appropriate Standards
- Willingness to Fail Forward

Crucial Checkpoints and Processes

- A Compelling Testimony
- A Passion to Multiply
- Process

Core Tools

- TUMI Capstone Curriculum
- TUMI Foundations Courses
- CTV Licensing
- CTV Ordination

FIT TO REPRESENT

Clear Goals

§3 FIT TO REPRESENT

Discipleship should have clear goals during each stage of growth. Having clear goals will help you prioritize and form their interactions with those you are leading in discipleship.

The Clear Goals in this stage of discipleship are:

1. **Discern, Train, Authorize, and Release**
2. **Empower the "Variety of Gifts"**
3. **Develop Disciples into the Next Generation of the Church**

1. Discern, Train, Authorize, and Release Emerging Leaders

As a leader you play a key role in the development of new leaders for the church. It will be your job to discern God's call on individuals' lives and train them to live into that calling. Knowing when to release a leader can be a challenging task, but you must be willing to authorize new servants to lead the church.

Discernment

You must constantly be alert and attentive to the signs of God's calling on a life, and be ready to respond with affirmation.

Training

Do not shrink from declaring and teaching anything that will be profitable, so that when the time comes you can confidently commend them to God and to the word of his grace (Acts 20.20, 32).

Authorization and Release

You must be willing to license and ordain new servants of the Lord. The formal public acknowledgment of emerging leaders is both honoring and empowering for them. Without lay hands on people too quickly, we should be generous with our authorization of new leaders.

2. Empower the "Variety of Gifts"

It is important to recognize that not everyone is a pastor or leader. This reality means that you must develop people in an open-ended way and trust the Lord for the results.

Even if someone does not show strong gifts in leadership, they are still important to the church and should be a valued member of your community. You must help everyone embrace the common call of the Great Commission and the value of every gift for spiritual reproduction. Some of the most important gifts to the life of a church or the success of a church plant are the less obvious ones like service, administration, hospitality, and generosity. In truth, these people will be the ones that create an atmosphere and a culture that makes new people feel welcomed and embraced.

3. Develop Disciples in the Next Generation of the Church

At this stage of discipleship you must ask, "What we are seeking for the future of the church and God's Kingdom?"

Am I seeking to establish and hold onto only my church?

If so, we will hold onto good people and keep them under us so that we can survive as a body.

Am I seeking to further Christ's kingdom only through our CTV churches?

If so, we will limit people's options and force CTV on them as if it were 'our way or the highway.'

Let us shamelessly seek the aggressive advance of God's kingdom everywhere!

We minister with real freedom that respects the authority of the Spirit to do what he will, when he will, with anyone he wills. If we do this, we will be free in the Holy Spirit to equip and empower disciples and leave calling and orchestrating things to the Lord. If we try to manage and control what God is doing, we will quickly find ourselves in danger of quenching the Holy Spirit in our church and in the lives of those we disciple. If we are kingdom-minded in our discipleship, the Lord will impact the world in ways we cannot imagine through our churches.

FIT TO REPRESENT

Critical Concepts and Perspectives

§3 FIT TO REPRESENT

The critical concepts and perspectives we must have in each stage of discipleship will help you view your discipleship process through the lens of what is most important for a new believer to learn and grow in.

The Clear Concepts and Perspectives We Must Have in this stage of discipleship are:

CONCEPTS

1. The Church as God's Army
2. Calling
3. Character
4. Competence
5. Community

PERSPECTIVES

1. The Sovereign Willing of the Spirit
2. Leaders make Leaders
3. High but Appropriate Standards
4. Willingness to Fail Forward

A Strong and Courageous Church

> ## CONCEPTS
> To train emerging leaders for kingdom advancement it is important to keep in mind a person's calling, character, competence, and community. The Spirit must lead and we must have high but appropriate standards.

1. The Church as God's Army

Emerging leaders have completely caught the vision of the church as God's army. They understand their place in the army and the job that God has called them to do to advance his kingdom. They are ready and willing to join the church in waging war against evil and darkness and declaring liberty to those still in bondage.

Biblical Images of Salvation and the Church

- **Captives set Free** (Acts 26.18) – We are liberated from the slavery of the hostile forces that oppose Christ (sin, death, and Satan).

- **Transfer of Kingdom Allegiance** (Colossians 1.13–14) – We have pledged allegiance to a new Lord, Jesus Christ, and have become citizens of his kingdom.

- **The Church Militant** (2 Corinthians 10.3–4) – We in turn declare liberty to the remaining captives, and wage war against the evil and darkness that continue to enslave humanity until the Lord's return!

The Implications of this Imagery

We are the agents of God's kingdom purposes and work in the world today, the very ambassadors of heaven in the world (Philippians 3.20–21). A leader lives this out in their own lives and engages others in the mission.

2. Calling

Christ is Lord and head of the church! By his mandate and leadership, he will direct people where he wants them to go. You must be sensitive to God's calling on people's lives and affirm in them what the Spirit is leading.

Discerning Calling – Hearing the mandate of the Lord

A key aspect of discipleship is being able to listen well, both to the individual and to the Holy Spirit. Some questions that may help you discern a person's calling could be:

- What is your burden?
- What do your opportunities to minister and your experiences say?
- What resonates with your heart?
- Where is there fruitfulness in the body?

Affirming Calling – Obeying the mandate of the Lord

You must respond to a believer's burdens and desires, but an equally crucial step in determining calling is listening to and obeying the Lord's leading. As a leader you must:

- Listen and observe in conversation with the Holy Spirit to discern his will.
- Give verbal affirmation and call out what the Lord is doing in a person.
- Entrust responsibility and authority, laying hands to commission people into new works of the Spirit.

3. Character

In order to represent Christ, we must *in fact* be conformed to his image by the Holy Spirit. The concern here is not information and learning, but deeds and life.

Evidencing the fruit of the Spirit (Galatians 5.22–23)

A mature disciple will evidence the fruit of the Spirit in their lives. No one is perfect, but the mark of a growing Christian is the increasing signs of love, joy, peace, patience, kindness, goodness, faithfulness, gentleness, and self-control.

Measures up to the Pauline standards of church leadership (1 Timothy 3.1–13; Titus 1.5–9)

In his Pastoral Letters, Paul gives some portraits of the character a church leader should embody. He paints a portrait of a person who exhibits godliness not only at church, but in their private life, their home life, their professional life, and their public life. True character is not a matter of putting on a show in one area. It is a pervasive reality seen in the total witness of a person's life.

4. Competence

We must walk by the power of the Holy Spirit and fulfill our appointed ministry with all of our might. The Spirit is the only one who can make us competent for ministry.

The particular emphasis here is competence in ministering to the people of God through the Word of God and prayer. It is reasonable for people to expect a leader in the church to know how to handle the Scriptures. Ministering the Word of God can take a variety of forms and is not limited to teaching and preaching. At every level, we desire that the Word of God would "dwell richly among us" (Colossians 3.16).

It is also reasonable for people to expect a godly leader to be a person of prayer. Leaders must obey Paul's call to consistent prevailing prayer (Romans 12.12; Ephesians 6.18; Philippians 4.6; Colossians 4.2; 1 Thessalonians 5.17, and others)

5. Community

Genuine Christian ministry is marked by a deep love for the Church and an unwavering commitment to serving God's people. A mature Christian evidences a genuine love for the brothers and sisters around them and ministers out of a sincere love for God's people and a desire to see them grow.

This love and commitment for God's people is what drives their ministry, not a desire for recognition or personal gain. A leader must model this self-sacrificing love for their disciples, teaching humility and commitment through example.

> **PERSPECTIVES WE MUST HAVE**
> As discipleship turns to training an emerging leader it is important to keep in mind that only disciples make disciples and emerging leaders need to embrace a warrior's mentality.

1. The Sovereign Willing of the Spirit (Acts 13.1-3)

It is the Spirit who truly leads, not us. The Spirit leads and moves according to God's purposes and our responsibility is to respond to his leading and not try to direct how he moves. As we allow the Spirit to guide our discipleship process, some important things to remember are:

- We can't force something that isn't there.

- We can't hold back something that is.

- We are authorized as leaders to recognize and confirm the Spirit's work, not to cause it or direct it.

2. Leaders make Leaders (2 Timothy 2.2)

Leadership development is not something different from the rest of the discipleship process. Just as mature godly disciples are indispensable to discipleship, so mature godly leaders are indispensable to training leaders. Tools and processes serve leaders as they raise up new leaders. The best leaders are not usually those who have read the most books or attended the most classes, but those who apprentice under good leaders. Be ready for emerging leaders to serve under you and learn how you do what you do.

3. High but Appropriate Standards (1 Timothy 3.1–13)

Lowering the standards of leadership is not good for the church and it's not good for leaders. In truth it helps no one. Your disciples should be held accountable to pursue excellence in their lives and ministry as they represent Christ and his church.

However, we must recognize appropriate standards and exercise wisdom to deal with the realities of life in an urban poor community. This may include issues such as a criminal history, messy marital and parental situations, and financial questions. We should not assume, for instance that a felony conviction or a past divorce automatically disqualifies someone from being a leader or a pastor. Our standards should allow for the Lord to call and empower people regardless of their past.

4. Willingness to Fail Forward

The fear of failure is the death of progress. A leader must be willing to fail forward as they pursue the mission in front of them. They should boldly pursue what they believe is from the Lord and let the success be up to the Lord.

You have to be willing to let people try, even if success is not certain. *Success will almost never be certain.* Discipling someone does not mean controlling every step they take or forcing people to do things exactly the way you would. Sometimes it means allowing others to make mistakes so that they can grow and learn.

FIT TO REPRESENT

Crucial Checkpoints and Processes

§3 FIT TO REPRESENT

At each stage of discipleship you should have clear checkpoints to use as benchmarks of growth and there should be specific steps worked into your discipleship plans.

The Crucial Checkpoints and Processes in this stage of discipleship are:

CHECKPOINTS

1. A Compelling Testimony
2. A Passion to Multiply

PROCESSES

1. Shared Responsibility
2. Apprenticeship
3. Classroom Training
4. Commissioning
5. Licensing and Ordination

CHECKPOINTS

It can often be difficult to know the appropriate time to release a leader into ministry. Here are a few checkpoints to look for in a mature leader. Taken from *Fit to Represent* (see appendix 2, p. 89).

1. A Compelling Testimony: Public Life and Vocation (1 Pet 3.15–16)

A mature leader is known by the testimony of their public life. They should be seen living out godly character in their own circles of influence and have a good reputation among their peers. Some important qualities you should see are:

- A God-honoring reputation

- Living a witnessing lifestyle

- Maintaining a good testimony in their *oikos* (family, friends, others in their circle of influence)

- Doing justice and loving mercy in their own circle

2. A Passion to Multiply: Evangelizing and Discipling through the Church (2 Timothy 2.1–2)

A mature leader has a passion to see the kingdom of God expand. Their vision should include leading the church to fulfill the Great Commission and their ministry objectives should include the following:

- Sharing the gospel with the lost

- Serving the neighbors, community, and beyond

- Helping new believers as they are welcomed and incorporated into the church

- Spiritual reproduction: involved in disciple-making

- A life committed to ministry and mission

PROCESSES

As you authorize and release new leaders for the church this checklist can serve as a process of key steps to include in your discipleship plan.

- ☑ Shared Responsibility – Reject the kind of specialization and professionalism that keep the lay/clergy distinction firmly in place. Open up the roles and functions in the church so that they become avenues of training, discovery, and growth.

- ☑ Apprenticeship – Match-up people who are clearly walking the same road.

- ☑ Classroom Training
    - ✓ TUMI Classes
    - ✓ Conferences
    - ✓ Other Courses or Programs

- ☑ Commissioning – Honor people who serve with ceremony and public affirmation.

- ☑ Licensing & Ordination

FIT TO REPRESENT

Core Tools
§3 FIT TO REPRESENT

At each stage of discipleship you should have go-to resources that will help you guide believers toward maturity.

Some Core Tools in this stage of discipleship are:

1. TUMI Capstone Curriculum
2. TUMI Foundations Courses
3. CTV Licensing
4. CTV Ordination

1. TUMI Capstone Curriculum

Capstone Curriculum is a 16-module training program, taught at a seminary level, specifically designed to serve as the most essential knowledge and skill learning necessary for effective urban ministry. As a complete training curriculum, it may be accessed through The Urban Ministry Institute's Satellite Certificate program. With this curriculum you will have everything you need to equip yourself and your leaders for effective ministry in your church and community. *For more information or to find a satellite location near you visit www.tumi.org.*

2. TUMI Foundations Courses

The Foundations for Ministry Series are resources of The Urban Ministry Institute (TUMI). The topics covered in these resources are foundational to effective urban ministry, and can be used by anyone seeking to equip leaders in urban churches and include seminars such as *Winning the World, Vision for Mission, The Gospel of John, Church Matters, Marking Time,* and many others. *TUMI Foundations courses are available through www.tumi.org.*

3. CTV Licensing

We should be ready to license those that the Lord is calling to function as a deacon or a ministry leader of some kind in a CTV church. Licensing is not a prerequisite to office of deacon, but should be sought by those who desire leadership in the church. This process of testing, formal acknowledgement, and authorization is a powerful tool in leadership development. *More on CTV Licensing can be found in the CTV Guidebook.*

4. CTV Ordination

We should also be ready to ordain new leader that the Lord is calling into works of church leadership, pastoral ministry, and church planting. Ordination is rigorous because it carries with it the full authorization to lead the church at the highest levels. Don't lower the standards for people on ordination. Instead equip and empower them to meet qualifications. Like licensing, this process of testing, formal acknowledgement, authorization, and release is a powerful tool in leadership development. *More on CTV Ordination can be found in the CTV Guidebook.*

APPENDICES

1	Over the Hump Chart	88
2	Fit to Represent Chart	89
3	Discerning the Call Chart	90
4	CTV Battle Cry	91
5	Nicene Creed: With Explanation and Biblical Support	93
6	The Story of God – Our Sacred Roots	97
7	Understanding the Church Year – A Guide to Colors, Themes, History, Etc.	101
8	Teaching the Lord's Prayer and Ten Commandments	109
9	Joshua as a Type of Christ	112

Appendix 1
Over the Hump

The Hump
Rev. Dr. Don L. Davis • Timothy 4.9-16; Hebrews 5.11-14

The Baby Christian
The New Believer and the Spiritual Disciplines

- Awkwardness
- Unskillfulness
- Mistakes
- Roughness
- Sporadic Behavior
- Uncomfortableness
- Inefficiency
- Novice-Level Performance

Heart Desire
A Clear Goal
Feasible Plan
Solid Support
Correct Knowledge
Faithful Effort
Good Examples
Extended Period of Time
Longsuffering

Regular, correct application of the spiritual disciplines

The Mature Christian
The Mature Believer and the Spiritual Disciplines

- Faithful Application
- Gracefulness
- Automatic response
- Comfortableness
- Personal Satisfaction
- Excellence
- Expertise
- Training Others

© 2004. The Urban Ministry Institute. All Rights Reserved. The Urban Ministry Institute is a ministry of World Impact, Inc.

Appendices

Appendix 2
Fit to Represent

Fit to Represent: Multiplying Disciples of the Kingdom of God
Rev. Dr. Don L. Davis

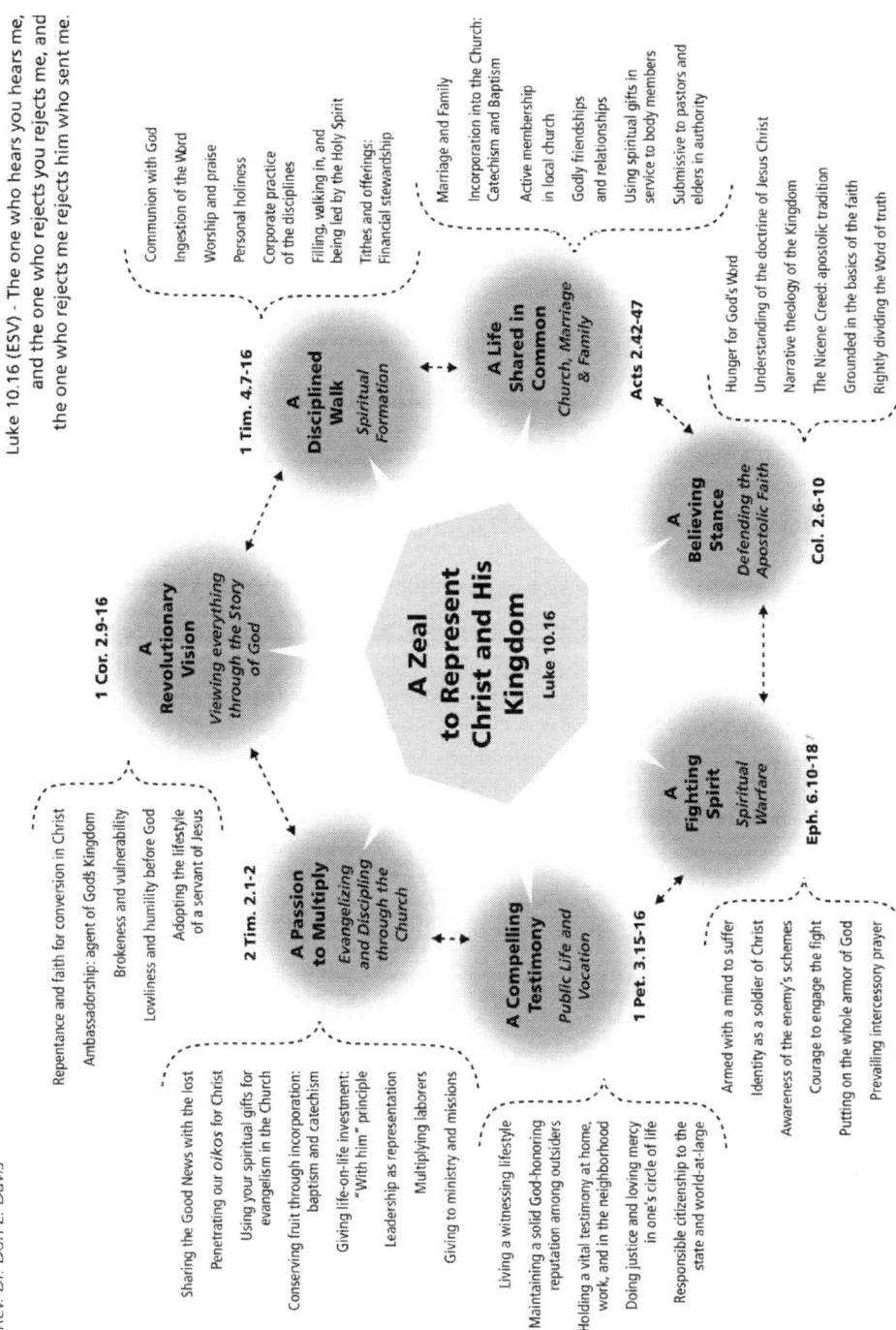

Luke 10.16 (ESV) - The one who hears you hears me, and the one who rejects you rejects me, and the one who rejects me rejects him who sent me.

A Zeal to Represent Christ and His Kingdom
Luke 10.16

A Disciplined Walk — *Spiritual Formation* — 1 Tim. 4.7-16
- Communion with God
- Ingestion of the Word
- Worship and praise
- Personal holiness
- Corporate practice of the disciplines
- Filling, walking in, and being led by the Holy Spirit
- Tithes and offerings: Financial stewardship

A Life Shared in Common — *Church, Marriage & Family* — Acts 2.42-47
- Marriage and Family
- Incorporation into the Church: Catechism and Baptism
- Active membership in local church
- Godly friendships and relationships
- Using spiritual gifts in service to body members
- Submissive to pastors and elders in authority

A Believing Stance — *Defending the Apostolic Faith* — Col. 2.6-10
- Hunger for God's Word
- Understanding of the doctrine of Jesus Christ
- Narrative theology of the Kingdom
- The Nicene Creed: apostolic tradition
- Grounded in the basics of the faith
- Rightly dividing the Word of truth

A Revolutionary Vision — *Viewing everything through the Story of God* — 1 Cor. 2.9-16

A Passion to Multiply — *Evangelizing and Discipling through the Church* — 2 Tim. 2.1-2
- Repentance and faith for conversion in Christ
- Ambassadorship: agent of God's Kingdom
- Brokenness and vulnerability
- Lowliness and humility before God
- Adopting the lifestyle of a servant of Jesus
- Sharing the Good News with the lost
- Penetrating our *oikos* for Christ
- Using your spiritual gifts for evangelism in the Church
- Conserving fruit through incorporation: baptism and catechism
- Giving life-on-life investment: "With him" principle
- Leadership as representation
- Multiplying laborers
- Giving to ministry and missions

A Compelling Testimony — *Public Life and Vocation* — 1 Pet. 3.15-16
- Living a witnessing lifestyle
- Maintaining a solid God-honoring reputation among outsiders
- Holding a vital testimony at home, work, and in the neighborhood
- Doing justice and loving mercy in one's circle of life
- Responsible citizenship to the state and world-at-large

A Fighting Spirit — *Spiritual Warfare* — Eph. 6.10-18
- Armed with a mind to suffer
- Identity as a soldier of Christ
- Awareness of the enemy's schemes
- Courage to engage the fight
- Putting on the whole armor of God
- Prevailing intercessory prayer

© 2002. The Urban Ministry Institute. All Rights Reserved. The Urban Ministry Institute is a ministry of World Impact, Inc.

Appendix 3
Discerning the Call

Discerning the Call: The Profile of a Cross-Cultural Urban Church Planter
Rev. Dr. Don L. Davis

	Commission	Character	Community	Competence
Definition	Recognizes the call of God and replies with prompt obedience to his lordship and leading	Reflects the character of Christ in his/her personal convictions, conduct, and lifestyle	Regards multiplying disciples in the body of Christ as the primary role of ministry	Responds in the power of the Spirit with excellence in carrying out their appointed tasks and ministry
Key Scripture	2 Tim. 1.6-14; 1 Tim. 4.14; Acts 1.8; Matt. 28.18-20	John 15.4-5; 2 Tim. 2.2; 1 Cor. 4.2; Gal. 5.16-23	Eph. 4.9-15; 1 Cor. 12.1-27	2 Tim. 2.15; 3.16-17; Rom. 15.14; 1 Cor. 12
Critical Concept	The Authority of God: God's leader acts on God's recognized call and authority, acknowledged by the saints and God's leaders	The Humility of Christ: God's leader demonstrates the mind and lifestyle of Christ in his or her actions and relationships	The Growth of the Church: God's leader uses all of his or her resources to equip and empower the body of Christ for his/her goal and task	The Power of the Spirit: God's leader operates in the gifting and anointed of the Holy Spirit
Central Elements	A clear call from God Authentic testimony before God and others Deep sense of personal conviction based on Scripture Personal burden for a particular task or people Confirmation by leaders and the body	Passion for Christlikeness Radical lifestyle for the Kingdom Serious pursuit of holiness Discipline in the personal life Fulfills role-relationships and bond-slave of Jesus Christ Provides an attractive model for others in their conduct, speech, and lifestyle (the fruit of the Spirit)	Genuine love for and desire to serve God's people Disciples faithful individuals Facilitates growth in small groups Pastors and equips believers in the congregation Nurtures associations and networks among Christians and churches Advances new movements among God's people locally	Endowments and gifts from the Spirit Sound discipling from an able mentor Skill in the spiritual disciplines Ability in the Word Able to evangelize, follow up, and disciple new converts Strategic in the use of resources and people to accomplish God's task
Satanic Strategy to Abort	Operates on the basis of personality or position rather than on God's appointed call and ongoing authority	Substitutes ministry activity and/or hard work and industry for godliness and Christlikeness	Exalts tasks and activities above equipping the saints and developing Christian community	Functions on natural gifting and personal ingenuity rather than on the Spirit's leading and gifting
Key Steps	Identify God's call Discover your burden Be confirmed by leaders	Abide in Christ Discipline for godliness Pursue holiness in all	Embrace God's Church Learn leadership's contexts Equip concentrically	Discover the Spirit's gifts Receive excellent training Hone your performance
Results	Deep confidence in God arising from God's call	Powerful Christlike example provided for others to follow	Multiplying disciples in the Church	Dynamic working of the Holy Spirit

© 2002. The Urban Ministry Institute. All Rights Reserved. The Urban Ministry Institute is a ministry of World Impact, Inc.

Appendix 4
CTV Battle Cry

Christ the Victor Churches *live* the victory of Jesus, *seek* the advance of his kingdom in the city, and *stand* on the ancient Christian faith.

*CTV **lives** the spectacular story of the victory of God's kingdom through Jesus Christ.*

The story of the Bible is the victory of God's kingdom through Jesus Christ.

The eternal God our Lord is the creator and ruler of all things. In pride, Satan rebelled against the Lord's reign and ignited a cosmic war. Human beings, created in God's own image, joined the rebellion by obeying Satan, the ancient serpent. God's world was plunged into darkness and subjected to sin and death. Yet, in his infinite mercy, the Lord promised to send a Savior to crush evil and redeem his creation. God sent his own Son, Jesus, down from heaven to invade the dark realm of Satan. Through Christ's life, death, resurrection, and ascension, the devil is defeated. When Jesus sat down at the right hand of the Father, he sent his Holy Spirit to empower us, the church, as we declare his victory in all the earth, and call everyone everywhere to flee the oppressive reign of the devil and to enter the blessed kingdom of his Son. Very soon, the Lord will completely conquer Satan and all demonic activity, and destroy sin and death, and he will establish his eternal kingdom. As followers of Christ, we are privileged to faithfully represent Christ as the Victor and coming King who destroys the works of the devil. The fight is on!

*CTV **seeks** a movement of churches that aggressively pursues the advance of God's kingdom by the power of the Holy Spirit.*

By the will and power of the Lord, Christ the Victor will be an unstoppable global movement of CTV churches, which declare and demonstrate the victory of the kingdom of God through Jesus Christ. We will experience warm fellowship and shared spirituality in vibrant churches of common identity and practice that confess and embody the richness and depth of the ancient Christian faith. We will empower the least in the world's eyes to be great in the kingdom of God. We will prayerfully and aggressively seek the advance of God's kingdom, stopping at nothing to win the hardest, darkest and poorest places in our cities for Christ.

*CTV **stands** on the ancient Christian faith as it has been believed and practiced everywhere, always, by all.*

- A shared spirituality centered on Christ and celebrated through the church year
- A historic theology anchored in Scripture and summarized by the Nicene Creed
- A focused mission committed to reproduction that results in indigenous church planting movements

Appendix 5
Nicene Creed with Explanation and Biblical Support

(*Italicized Verses* are recommended for memorization)

We believe in one God, (Deuteronomy 6.4–5, Mark 12.29, 1 Corinthians 8.6)
> *There is one living and true God, infinitely perfect in glory, wisdom, holiness, justice, power and love, one in his essence but eternally existing in three persons: God the Father, God the Son and God the Holy Spirit.*

the Father Almighty, (Genesis 17.1, Daniel 4.35, Matthew 6.9, Ephesians 4.6, Revelation 1.8)

> *God is the Almighty One. He is completely free from restriction or limitation. The Almighty reveals himself to us as a gracious and compassionate Father who loves the world.*

maker of heaven and earth, (Genesis 1.1, Isaiah 40.28, Revelation 10.6)
of all things visible and invisible. (Psalm 148, Romans 11.36, Hebrews 11.3, Revelation 4.11)

> *From eternity past our Triune God existed in perfect joy. He alone is uncreated. As the sovereign Lord, he created all that exists out of nothing and reigns as the one true king of all. In blasphemous pride, Satan rebelled against the Lord's reign and ignited a cosmic war. Human beings, created in God's own image, joined the rebellion by obeying Satan, the ancient serpent. God's world was plunged into darkness and subjected to sin and death.*

We believe in one Lord Jesus Christ, the only begotten Son of God, begotten of the Father before all ages, God from God, Light from Light, true God from true God, begotten, not created, of the same essence as the Father, (John 1.1–2, 3.16–18, 8.58, 14.9–10, 20.28, Colossians 1.15–17, Hebrews 1.3–6)

> *In the Trinity none is before or after the others; none is greater or less than another; but the whole three Persons are coeternal together, and coequal. God the Son, who in his incarnation is Jesus of Nazareth, shares in total equality the nature and position of the Father and the Spirit. His status as only begotten Son in no way implies that he is a subordinate or created being.*

Through whom all things were made. (John 1.3, Colossians 1.16)

Jesus is the Word of God made flesh. God created by the power of his word alone. Everything that exists came into being through the Son, the Word of God.

Who for us men and for our salvation came down from heaven and was incarnate by the Holy Spirit and the Virgin Mary, and became human. (Matthew 1.20–23, John 1.14, 6.38, Luke 19.10, 1 John 3.8)

In the fullness of time, Jesus Christ, the eternal Son, became human without ceasing to be God by uniting to his divine nature a true human nature in his incarnation, and so continues to be both God and man, in two distinct natures and one person, forever. The two natures exist in one person without confusion, without change, without division, and without separation. He was conceived by the Holy Spirit and born of the Virgin Mary. He came down from heaven as the champion to invade the dark realm of the evil one. He exhibited the presence of God's kingdom in his person through manifold miracles.

Who for us too was crucified under Pontius Pilate, suffered and was buried. (Matthew 27.1–2, Mark 15.24–39, 15.43–47, Acts 13.29, Romans 5.8, 1 Corinthians 15.3–4, Colossians 2.13–15, Hebrews 2.10)

Jesus of Nazareth, the Word made flesh, suffered, died, and was buried. He lived a perfectly sinless life and died as the sacrifice for the sin of the whole world. His shed blood is the vicarious and propitiatory atonement for human sin. He is the only way that we can find salvation and reconciliation with God.

The third day he rose again according to the Scriptures, (Mark 16.5–7, Luke 24.6–8, Acts 1.3, Romans 6.9, 10.9, 1 Corinthians 15.4–6, 2 Timothy 2.8)

The same Jesus who died was truly and bodily raised from the dead on the third day. He appeared to the disciples and to many believers, proving himself to be alive with various signs. His resurrection proves his victory over sin, death, and Satan and opens the way for us to receive eternal life in his kingdom.

ascended into heaven and is seated at the right hand of the Father. (Luke 24.50–53, Acts 1.9–11, 7.55–56, Ephesians 1.19–20)

Jesus ascended into heaven while the disciples looked on, sat down at the right hand of the Father, and now intercedes in glory for his redeemed as our great high priest and advocate, and as the head of the church and Lord of the individual believer.

Appendices

He will come again in glory to judge the living and the dead, and his kingdom will have no end. (Isaiah 9.7, Matthew 24.30, Luke 1.33, John 5.22, Acts 1.11, Romans 14.9, 2 Corinthians 5.10, 2 Timothy 4.1)

> *One day very soon, the Lord Jesus Christ will return bodily, visibly and personally to receive his own, to conform believers to his own image. He will complete the victory initially won at the cross, utterly destroying Satan, all demonic activity, sin, and death, and establishing his eternal kingdom. He will judge the living and the dead and will effect a final separation of the redeemed and the lost, assigning unbelievers to eternal punishment and believers to eternal glory, enjoying conscious fellowship with him.*

We believe in the Holy Spirit, the Lord and life-giver, (Genesis 1.1–2, Job 33.4, Psalm 104.30, Luke 4.18–19, John 3.5–6, 16.7–11, 1 Corinthians 2.11, 2 Corinthians 3.17, Revelation 3.22)

> *The Holy Spirit convicts the world of sin, righteousness and judgment; through the ministry of regeneration and sanctification applies salvation and places believers into the church, guides and comforts God's children, indwells, directs, gifts and empowers the church in godly living and service in order to fulfill the Great Commission, and seals and keeps the believer until Christ returns.*

who proceeds from the Father and the Son, (John 14.16–18, 14.26, 15.26, 20.22)

> *When Jesus ascended to the right hand of the Father, he sent his Holy Spirit to indwell his church at Pentecost. Through the indwelling of the Holy Spirit, God is present in the church and in the individual believer.*

who together with the Father and the Son is worshipped and glorified, (Isaiah 6.3, Matthew 28.19, 2 Corinthians 13.14, Revelation 4.8)

> *As an equal member of the Trinity, the Spirit is equally deserving of worship and glory. We should neither ignore the Spirit, nor emphasize the Spirit over the Father and the Son.*

who spoke by the prophets. (Numbers 11.29, Acts 2.17–18, 2 Timothy 3.16–17, 2 Peter 1.21)

> *The sixty-six books which form the canon of the Old and New Testaments are verbally inspired by God, inerrant in the original writings, the only infallible rule of faith and practice.*

We believe in one holy catholic and apostolic church. (Matthew 16.18, Ephesians 4.4–6, 5.25–28, 1 Corinthians 1.2, 10.17, 1 Timothy 3.15, Revelation 7.9)

> *The holy church is the one institution specifically ordained of God to function in the furthering of the kingdom until Christ comes again. It consists of all those regenerated by the Spirit of God, in mystical union and communion both with Christ, the head of the body, and with fellow-believers. Neighborhood congregations are the local manifestation of the church universal. In obedience to the command of Christ, these congregations preach the Word of God, equip God's people for the work of ministry, and administer the sacraments of baptism and communion.*

We acknowledge one baptism for the forgiveness of sin, (Acts 2.38–39, 22.16, 1 Peter 3.21, Ephesians 4.4–5)

> *Every person, regardless of race or rank, who receives the Lord Jesus Christ by faith is born into the family of God and receives eternal life. This occurs solely because of the grace of God and has no ground in human merit. Water baptism is the believer's incorporation into the visible body of Christ and a pledge to renounce sin and evil, to die to ourselves, and to live under the lordship of Jesus Christ as a part of his church.*

and we look for the resurrection of the dead and the life of the age to come. (Isaiah 11.6–10, Luke 18.29–30, 1 Corinthians 15.22–25, Revelation 21.1–5, 21.22–22.5)

> *One day, at the return of our Lord, all the dead in Christ will be resurrected to everlasting life. Those who are alive at his coming will be changed from mortality to immortality. Our eternal dwelling will be with God in a new heaven and a new earth, free from the devil, death, pain, sin, and curse of our present world. We will live with him in eternal bliss and perfect communion.*

Amen.

Appendix 6
The Story of God – Our Sacred Roots

In his book, *Sacred Roots: A Primer for Retrieving the Great Tradition* (The Urban Ministry Institute, 2010), Dr. Don Davis lays out an excellent paradigm for understanding the story of God as it has been understood by the church throughout history. "In drawing from this rich well of the church's history, we discern eight interconnected themes which gave the ancient undivided church its amazing vitality, clarity, and strength during troubled times" (*Sacred Roots*, 75). Christ the Victor uses the *Sacred Roots* paradigm as our grid for retrieving the Great Tradition and living the story of God in Christ.

The Story of God in Two Parts

One of the most insightful features of Dr. Davis' paradigm is the distinction between the *objective foundation* and the *subjective response* of the story. The church is a dependent entity. As Christians, you and I exist only as a response and participation to the person and work of the Triune God. The salvation of the church is an extremely important part of the story, and in some ways, defines the way in which God goes about his work. It is however, secondary to the central story of the victory of the kingdom of God through Jesus Christ. The foundational reality of the story is the truth of who God is and what he is doing to destroy evil and bring redemption. Everything about our existence depends on and issues from him.

A Framework for Everything

The *Sacred Roots* paradigm clearly identifies fours ways in which you can easily understand our participation in the story. The categories laid out here form the thinking behind everything CTV does. Anything we might want to say about the church or the Christian life fits somewhere in this paradigm.

This paradigm fundamentally shapes everything about CTV. *The Story of God* is the world in which we live. The objective story of the person and work of the triune God as told in Scripture is the essence of our identity and our worldview. The subjective responses of the church are the substance of our churches. The identity of CTV (*The Banner We Raise*) is specifically crafted to fill out these four responses. In some ways, this book is designed to show how these four responses define our identity and how they are lived throughout the life of a church. The following is adapted from *Sacred Roots*, pp.75–83.

The Objective Foundation: The Triune God's Unfolding Drama[3]

"God is telling his own Story and acting in his own unfolding drama, a true tale which culminates in the person and work of Jesus Christ" (*Sacred Roots*, 75). The person and work of the triune God as revealed in Scripture are the objective foundation of the story. He is always working to bring about his sovereign and gracious will. You and I are always in the position of responding to God's actions. The central plotline of this unfolding drama is *the victory of the kingdom of God's Kingdom through Jesus Christ*.

The Alpha and Omega

The Triune God is the Alpha and Omega, the beginning and the end. He is the eternal God, the true creator and ruler of all things. Even though human beings joined the devil in rebellion against God's rule, he graciously promised to crush evil and redeem humanity from the tyranny of sin, death, and Satan. In his great love, the Father determined to save through his Son a people that would bring him eternal glory. One day soon he will destroy evil forever, make a new heaven and earth, and dwell with his people forever.

Christus Victor

In the fullness of time, God sent his own Son, Jesus, down from heaven to invade the dark realm of Satan. The Son took on flesh being born of a virgin, and he became human. He lived without sin in order to be the spotless sacrifice for the sin of humanity. Through Christ's life, death, and resurrection the devil is defeated and sin and death are overcome. He ascended to the right hand of the Father where he waits for all his enemies to be put under his feet. Before he left, he promised to return and finish the victory of God's kingdom forever.

Come, Holy Spirit

When Christ left, he sent God the Holy Spirit to be with his church. The Spirit indwells every true follower of Jesus, creating new life in us, baptizing us into the one body, sealing us for redemption, gifting us for service, and empowering us for ministry. He unites the church and expands the kingdom of God as Christians keep in step with him. Through the power of the indwelling Spirit, the church is enabled to represent Christ by proclaiming his victory to all people everywhere and manifesting his power to destroy the works of the devil.

---

[3] Sacred Roots images – © 2009. The Urban Ministry Institute. All Rights Reserved. For more information on Sacred Roots, please visit www.tumi.org.

Your Word is Truth[4]

The Scriptures bear witness to the person and work of the Triune God, and ensure the faithful preservation of the story of God. Through the prophets and apostles, God has given a record of his mighty saving acts in history, and the promise of his future kingdom work. The Scriptures are God-breathed and are without fault or error. The Holy Spirit, who inspired the Scriptures, illumines them for the church, revealing Jesus as their center, theme, and subject. Through them, he also gives the church the power to declare and demonstrate the gospel of Jesus Christ.

The Subjective Response: The Church's Participation in God's Unfolding Drama

The church responds to and participates in the scriptural witness of the person and work of the triune God through theology, worship, discipleship, and mission. We find our identity, meaning, and purpose as the people of God only in relationship to the unfolding drama of the victory of the kingdom of God through Jesus Christ.

The Great Confession

We are the people of the story. The church believes and bears witness to the story revealed by God in Scripture. The Nicene Creed serves as a summary of the truth of Scripture and a rule of faith for all who bear the name of Christ. This creed is the clearest summary of the Christian faith as it has been believed everywhere, always, by all. It is our job to confess, understand, explain, and defend this rule of faith.

His Life in Us

We retell and reenact the story in our worship. We are priests of the Lord who offer him the spiritual sacrifice of praise for the glory of God. Through the weekly liturgy of the Word and the Table, spiritual songs, and community prayer we experience fellowship with the triune God and receive grace and strength to follow our King. Through the church year, we walk with Christ through his life, death, resurrection, ascension, and eventual return. His life becomes the pattern of our shared life.

---

[4] Sacred Roots images – © 2009. The Urban Ministry Institute. All Rights Reserved. For more information on Sacred Roots, please visit www.tumi.org.

Living in the Way[5]

We embody the story as we live in the way of Christ. The Lord longs to shape us into the image of Christ both corporately and individually. Through a rich shared spirituality we open ourselves to his transforming grace. We live the baptized life united with Jesus through the Holy Spirit. We walk the path of the church year together as a community. We participate in shared disciplines that focus our daily lives on Christ. We take up the full armor of God as we fight the spiritual battle with strength and courage.

Reborn to Serve

We continue the story. In his grace and mercy, the Lord has chosen us to represent him in the earth. We are his body and we live to carry out the goals, priorities, lifestyle, and deeds of our Head, Jesus Christ. We are called by him to be agents of the kingdom of God in the world, especially among the poor. We humbly serve and sacrifice for the sake of the gospel following the example of Jesus our Lord.

Christ the Victor intentionally seeks to retrieve the Great Tradition. We believe that the cities will be won to Christ as together we train, authorize and release men, women, boys, and girls who God raises up from the least-expected places to be dynamic leaders for the local church in the city. *Sacred Roots* offers a clear way to train urban disciples and can help ignite and sustain an urban church planting movement. It is our conviction that the *Sacred Roots* paradigm can provide the church with a powerful sense of her true identity as the body and bride of Christ, and can be used to empower urban disciples with the tools they need to lead and multiply churches among the urban poor.

---

[5] Sacred Roots images – © 2009. The Urban Ministry Institute. All Rights Reserved. For more information on Sacred Roots, please visit www.tumi.org.

Appendix 7
Understanding the Church Year – A Guide to Colors, Themes, History, Etc.

Understanding the Seasons

The seasons and observances follow the outline of the life and ministry of Jesus, allowing us to tread in his footsteps year after year.

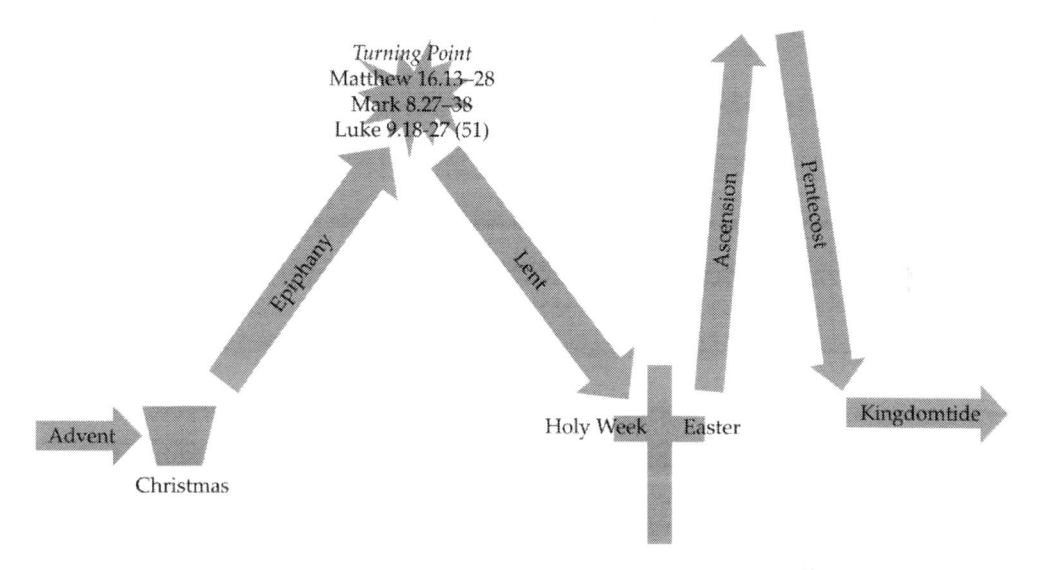

Turning Point
Matthew 16.13–28
Mark 8.27–38
Luke 9.18-27 (51)

Epiphany · Lent · Ascension · Pentecost

Advent · Christmas · Holy Week · Easter · Kingdomtide

Advent – *The Anticipation of Christ*

> *Name:* Latin for 'Coming' or 'Arrival'
>
> *Emphasis:* We recall the days prior to the first coming of Christ and repent as we look forward to his second coming.
>
> *Colors:* Purple – Royalty, Repentance (Weeks 1, 2, 4); Pink – Joy, Happiness (Week 3)

Christmas – *The Birth of Christ*

> *Name:* Originally 'The Christ Mass', or the service celebrating incarnation of Christ (The term Mass is from the Old English for 'dismissal' and was likely the final word of the church service.)
>
> *Emphasis:* We celebrate that God the Son became flesh by the Holy Spirit and the Virgin Mary and dwelt among us.
>
> *Color:* Gold – Majesty, Glory

Epiphany – *The Manifestation of Christ*

Name: Greek for 'Manifestation'

Emphasis: We affirm that in Jesus of Nazareth, the kingdom of God is shining its light into the dark realm of the devil.

Colors: Green – Hope, Life; Gold – Majesty, Glory (The Epiphany, Transfiguration Sunday)

Lent – *The Lowliness of Christ*

Name: Short for Lenten, from the Old English for 'Springtime'.

Emphasis: We take up the cross and walk with Christ the path of complete humility and servanthood.

Colors: Purple – Royalty, Repentance

Holy Week – *The Suffering and Death of Christ*

Name: Traditionally the final three days are called the *Paschal Triduum*, which means the three days related to our Passover.

Emphasis: We share in the sufferings and death of Christ in order that we may be raised to new life in him.

Colors: Purple – Royalty, Repentance; Black – Mourning, Death (Good Friday, Holy Saturday)

Easter – *The Resurrection of Christ*

Name: Historically called *Pascha* from the Greek for Passover; Easter was adapted from the name of an ancient English month equivalent to April.

Emphasis: We shout for joy because Jesus is risen from the dead and seated at the right hand of the Father; Christ is the victor over sin, death, and Satan!

Colors: Gold – Majesty, Glory

Appendices

Pentecost – *The Coming of the Holy Spirit*

Name: From the Greek for '50'; the Holy Spirit arrived 50 days after the resurrection.

Emphasis: We remember that the arrival of the Holy Spirit on the church means new life and amazing power to declare and demonstrate the victory of Christ to the ends of the earth.

Colors: Red – Holy Spirit as a Fire

Kingdomtide (Ordinary Time) – *A Season of Christ's Headship, Harvest, and Hope*

Name: The suffix 'tide' is Old English for a period of time. Kingdomtide then is the time of the advance of the kingdom. Ordinary means numbered (as in ordinal numbers 1st, 2nd, 3rd, etc.).

Emphasis: In these last days the Spirit-filled church submits to the headship of Christ our Lord, labors for the harvest of Christ our Savior, and prepares the way for the second coming of Christ our King.

Colors: Gold – Majesty, Glory (Trinity Sunday, Reign of Christ the King); Green – Hope, Life; Red – Blood of the Martyrs (All Saints' Day)

Understanding the Calendar

1. The Date of Easter – The First Council of Nicaea (325) established the date of Easter as the first Sunday after the full moon following the northern hemisphere's vernal equinox. This Sunday always falls between 3/22–4/25.

2. Dependent Celebrations – A 90-day Moving Block

    a. Ash Wednesday – 40 Days Before Easter

    b. Ascension Day – 40 Days After Easter, but is usually celebrated the Sunday before Pentecost (6th Sunday of Easter)

    c. Pentecost – 50 Days After Easter (7th Sunday of Easter)

3. Epiphany and Kingdomtide adjust on either side to compensate.

      a. Weeks 6–8 of Epiphany = Propers 1–3 of Kingdomtide

      b. Epiphany can be as short as five Sundays, or as long as nine. The last Sunday always celebrates the Transfiguration of Christ.

      c. Kingdomtide can begin anywhere between Propers 1–9. The first Sunday of Kingdomtide is always Trinity Sunday.

Understanding the History and Development of the Church Year

1. The Jewish Liturgical Calendar

   a. The church year has its roots in the Jewish festival calendar laid out by the Lord in the Old Testament.

   b. The Lord designed for his people, Israel, a program of shared spiritual formation that included regular observances, festivals, feasts, and fasts.

   c. Sabbath – The Foundation of the Calendar

      i. Weekly Saturday Rest – 7 Day Cycle

      ii. Sabbatical Year Rest – 7 Year Cycle

      iii. Year of Jubilee – 7x7 Year Cycle

   d. Major Seasonal Observances (see Leviticus 23)

      i. Feast of Passover/Unleavened Bread (Mid-April) – Re-enactment of the night before the great Exodus; all males required to appear in Jerusalem.

      ii. Feast of Pentecost/Weeks/First-fruits (7 Weeks after Passover, Early June) – Celebration of the first-fruits of the harvest, and remembrance of the giving of the Law at Sinai; all males required to appear in Jerusalem.

Appendices

      iii. Feast of Trumpets (Early October) – Civil New Year [*Rosh Hashanah*]

      iv. The Day of Atonement [Yom Kippur] (Mid-October) – High holy day of the Israelite year; a solemn fast, and day of repentance, where the high priest enters into the Holy of Holies and cleanses both the nation and the temple from sin.

      v. Feast of Tabernacles (Late October) – Marks the completion of the harvest, and remembers the wandering of Israel in the desert; all males required to appear in Jerusalem.

   e. Seasonal Observances Added Later

      i. Festival of Purim (Mid-March) – Originates in the mid 400's B.C. It celebrates the deliverance of the Jews narrated in the book of Esther.

      ii. Festival of Lights [*Hanukkah*] (Late December) – Originated in 164 B.C.; Celebrates the rededication of the Temple beginning the brief period where the Jewish Maccabees ruled in Judea.

2. Early Jewish Christianity

   a. The earliest Christians thought of themselves as essentially Jewish (see Acts 2.46, 3.1, 5.20,42, 11.26 [It is not until here that a new name, 'Christian,' is used to describe them.]).

   b. The Jewish festival calendar centered on two foci – The Exodus and the harvest.

   c. Building on the God-ordained festival calendar, the early church began to reshape the liturgical year in light of the coming of the prophesied Messiah, who brought the new Exodus, and who calls us into a new harvest.

d. Saturday Sabbath → Sunday, The Lord's Day (in honor of the day of Christ's resurrection; see Acts 20.7; 1 Corinthians 16.2; Revelation 1.10)

e. Passover → Easter (1 Corinthians 5.7–8)

f. Pentecost, Festival of First-fruits of the Wheat Harvest → Pentecost, the Celebration of the coming of the Holy Spirit bringing in the First-fruits of the great Spiritual Harvest.

3. The Development of the Church Year

   a. The weekly Sunday celebration (centering on hearing the Word, and taking communion) and the yearly celebration of Easter in place of Passover have legitimate claim to originating in the time of the biblical Apostles.

   b. Pentecost is celebrated with a distinct Christian emphasis in the earliest post-Apostolic time, likely the 100's. This development constitutes the first season of the church year, the 50 days of the Easter season.

   c. The other major seasons are added over the next 200 years.

      i. Advent – A period of preparation for the nativity of Christ is in place by the mid-300's. The length of this time, however, varied from 3 weeks to 40 days until the 500's when Gregory the Great fixed it at 4 weeks.

      ii. Christmas & Epiphany – These two celebrations are closely linked. Originally, Easter celebrated "the entire mystery of Christ including the incarnation with the moment of conception, which put the nativity nine months later" (Cobb, 467). These seasons were likely united in their origin. The first clear reference to these as yearly celebrations of the church comes in 361. The ancient festival celebrated the nativity, the visit of the Magi, the baptism, and the first miracle of Jesus (the Miracle at

Cana). Christmas likely becomes independent of Epiphany in the early 300's.

   iii. Lent – The first mention of Lent is at the Council of Nicaea (325), although it was widely known and accepted by then. This likely puts its origin in the 200's.

   iv. Holy Week – Palm Sunday was reenacted yearly in Jerusalem as early as the 300's, and was imitated in other places starting in the 400's. The Paschal Triduum originated around this same time.

d. Other observances are added by the church as the centuries passed.

   i. All Saints' Day – As early as the 400's Christians celebrated a day honoring the martyrs of the church. In 609/10, the church made All Saints' Day an official celebration of the church year.

   ii. Trinity Sunday – Originates as a grassroots celebration in the 1000's, and is officially mandated as part of the church year in the 1300's.

   iii. Christ the King – Instituted in 1925 to combat nationalism following World War I. Many Christians were displaying a loyalty to countries and leaders that eclipsed their loyalty to Christ and his church.

   Note: Other forms of the church year include celebrations for various people and events on almost every day of the year.

e. Lectionaries developed alongside the church year as a schedule of appropriate readings for the days and seasons.

   i. Jewish tradition actually suggests that readings were associated with certain festivals and days in the time of Moses.

ii. Whether that Jewish tradition is true or not, it is clear that lectionaries existed in Judaism during the second temple period (516 B.C.E. – A.D. 70). The Christian use of lectionaries seems to have been inherited from Judaism.

Appendix 8
Teaching the Lord's Prayer and Ten Commandments

The Lord's Prayer (Matthew 6.9–13, ESV)

Our Father in heaven,
Hallowed be your name;
Your kingdom come, your will be done on earth as it is in heaven;
Give us this day our daily bread;
And forgive us our debts, as we also have forgiven our debtors;
And lead us not into temptation, but deliver us from evil;
For yours is the kingdom and the power and the glory forever.
Amen[6]

Explanation of the Parts of the Lord's Prayer

- *Our Father in heaven* – Recognition of the Lord: We recognize the gracious character and exalted position of the One we address.

- *Hallowed be your name* – God's Glory: We acknowledge the Lord as holy (hallowed), ask Him to make his glory (his name) known and recognized on the earth.

- *Your kingdom come, your will be done on earth as it is in heaven* – Desire for God's Purposes: We ask God to fulfill his purposes and plans on the earth, and we submit to his will for us. We declare our trust in God's goodness and control, and bring requests for the expansion of his kingdom rule.

- *Give us this day our daily bread* – Dependence on God's Provision: We recognize that all of us depend on the Lord for everything, even the most basic needs, and bring requests of provision to God on behalf of others and ourselves.

- *And forgive us our debts, as we also have forgiven our debtors* – Our Repentance and Kingdom Relationships: We recognize that we are

---

[6] In the ESV, the phrase "For yours is the kingdom and the power and the glory, forever. Amen" appears in the footnote of Matthew 6.13.

sinners who depend on the grace and mercy of the Lord. We confess our sins, and ask for help in extending God's grace and mercy to others.

- *And lead us not into temptation, but deliver us from evil* – Our Purity and Protection: We ask the Lord to protect us from Satan's attempts to derail us in sin, and to harm us physically and spiritually.

- *For yours is the kingdom and the power and the glory forever, Amen* – Our Submission: We submit ourselves to the fact that the earth is the Lord's, and everything in it, all glory and honor are due him; we claim none for ourselves but give it all to him.

Ten Commandments

Exodus 20.1–17 & Deuteronomy 5.6–21

1. You shall have no other gods before me.

2. You shall not make for yourself an idol, whether in the form of anything that is in heaven above, or that is on the earth beneath, or that is in the water under the earth. You shall not bow down to them or worship them.

3. You shall not make wrongful use of the name of the Lord your God.

4. Observe the Sabbath day and keep it holy, as the Lord your God commanded you. Six days you shall labor and do all your work. But the seventh day is a Sabbath to the Lord your God.

5. Honor your father and your mother.

6. You shall not murder.

7. You shall not commit adultery.

8. You shall not steal.

9. You shall not bear false witness against your neighbor.

10. You shall not covet your neighbor's wife. Neither shall you desire your neighbor's house, or field, or male or female slave, or ox, or donkey, or anything that belongs to your neighbor.

Appendices

Ethical Application[7]

Commandment	Ethical Application
1) Have no other gods. Ex. 20.2–3 Deut. 5.6–7	God should be our top priority and final authority. We owe him alone our worship and obedience.
2) Make no idols or images of gods. Ex. 20.4–6 Deut. 5.8–10	Worship must reflect a proper view of God. It cannot be manipulative or self-serving.
3) Do not misuse of the name of the Lord. Ex. 20.7 Deut. 5.11	We must take our commitment to God seriously and not treat him, or his name, as something common and ordinary.
4) Observe the Sabbath. Ex. 20.8–11 Deut. 5.12–15	We must trust the Lord in everything, rather than ourselves, our effort, or our work. We can display this by taking a regular day to rest from work.
5) Honor your father and mother. Ex. 20.12 Deut. 5.16	We must recognize that the authorities in our lives were placed there by God and respect them, especially our family.
6) Do not murder. 7) Do not adultery. 8) Do not steal. Ex. 20.13–15 Deut. 5.17–19	We must respect the dignity of human beings, particularly their lives, families, and property.
9) Do not give false witness. Ex. 20.16 Deut. 5.20	We must be honest and faithful to our word.
10) Do not covet. Ex. 20.17 Deut. 5.21	We must accept what the Lord has given us without being jealous of others.

---

[7] Adapted from *Chronological and Background Charts of the Old Testament* by John Walton (Zondervan, 1994, p.24).

Appendix 9
Joshua as a Type of Christ
Terry Cornett, M.A., M.A.R.,

> The word "type" is used to denote a resemblance between something present (a person, object, or event) and something future. Typology is a method of biblical interpretation whereby an element found in the Old Testament is seen to prefigure one found in the New Testament. St. Paul uses this approach to Bible interpretation in 1 Corinthians 10:1-11.

> *(Heb. 4:6-8 ESV) Since therefore it remains for some to enter it and those who formerly received the good news failed to enter because of disobedience, again he appoints a certain day, "Today," saying through David so long afterward, in the words already quoted, "Today, if you hear his voice, do not harden your hearts." For if Joshua had given them rest, God would not have spoken of another day later on.*

All the elect foretold this Morning Star; they were His forerunners by their holy lives, and they prophesied about Him by word and deed. In fact, there was not a single just person who was not figuratively His herald. –St. Gregory the Great (Church Father, Doctor of the Church, and Saint, 540 AD – 604 AD)

Jesus [that is Joshua] son of Nun, in many ways offers us a figure (typos) of Christ. It was from the time of the crossing of the Jordan that he began to exercise his command of the people: this is where Christ also, having first been baptized, began His public life. The son of Nun established twelve (men) to divide the inheritance: Jesus sent twelve apostles into the whole world as heralds of the truth. He who is the figure saved Rahab the prostitute because she believed; He who is the reality said: 'The publicans and prostitutes will go before you in the kingdom of God.' The walls of Jericho fell at the mere sound of the trumpets at the time of the type; and because of the word of Jesus: 'there shall not remain one stone upon a stone,' – the temple of Jerusalem is fallen before our eyes." –St. Cyril of Jerusalem (Church Father, Doctor of the Church, and Saint, 313 AD – 386 AD)

The name of Jesus (Joshua) was a type. . . . .But this man was on this account so called as a type; for he used to be called Hoshea. Therefore the name was changed: for it was a prediction and a prophecy. He brought in the people into the promised land, as Jesus [brought them] into heaven" –St. John Chrysostom

Appendices

(Church Father, Doctor of the Church, and Saint, 347 AD – 407 AD)

Joshua, however, denotes Christ, because of his name and because of what he does. Although he was a servant of Moses, yet after his master's death he leads the people in and parcels out the inheritance of the Lord. Thus Christ, who was first made under the Law (Gal. 4:4), served it for us; then, when it was ended, He established another ministry, that of the Gospel, by which we are led through Him into the spiritual kingdom of a conscience joyful and serene in God, where we reign forever. –Martin Luther (Protestant Reformer, 1483 AD -- 1586 AD)

Joshua must be herein a type of Christ, who has not only conquered the gates of hell for us, but has opened to us the gates of heaven, and having purchased the eternal inheritance for all believers, will put them in possession of it. –Matthew Henry (English Presbyterian Minister, 1662 AD – 1714 AD)

Now, first, as is very obvious, Joshua is a type of our Lord Jesus Christ, as regards his name; for Joshua is in Hebrew what Jesus is in Greek. When we think what high things are told us in the New Testament concerning the Name of Jesus, what reverence towards it is enjoined us, and what virtue is ascribed to it, who can doubt that it is a very significant circumstance indeed, that the successor of Moses should bear it? This circumstance leads us from the first to expect that the history of Joshua will contain much in it bearing upon the blessed times of the Gospel. –Cardinal John Henry Newman (Roman Catholic Cardinal, 1801 AD – 1890 AD)

JOSHUA (*Yehoshua*)	**JESUS (*Yeshua*--short form of *Yehoshua*)**
A descendant of the patriarch Joseph [through Ephraim] (1Ch. 7:20-27)	The [adopted] son of Joseph the carpenter (Joh. 1:45)
Name means "The Lord (YHWH) Saves"	Name means "The Lord (YHWH) Saves"
He was the successor to Moses (Deu. 31:14, Jos. 1:1-2)	He was the successor to Moses (Joh. 5:46, Act. 3:22, Heb. 3:1-6, Rev. 15:3)
Spent 40 years in the wilderness preparing for leadership (Deu. 8:2)	Spent 40 days in the wilderness preparing for leadership (Mat. 4:1-2, Luk. 4:1-2)
God was "with him" (Jos. 1:5)	Called "God with us" [Immanuel]

	(Mat. 1:23)
God exalted him (Jos. 3:7)	God exalted Him (Act. 5:31, Php. 2:9)
The Holy Spirit rested on him (Num. 27:18)	The Holy Spirit rested on Him (Joh. 1:32)
Remained in the House of God (Exo. 33:11)	Remained in the House of God (Luk. 2:49)
Performed miracles involving power over nature (Jos. 3:10-17, 6:20, 10:8-11, 10:12-14)	Performed miracles involving power over nature (Mat. 8:23-27, Mar. 6:47-50, Mar. 11:20-21)
Purged greed from God's people (Jos. 7:16-25)	Purged greed from God's people (Joh. 2:13-16)
Jewish intertestamental literature calls him: • Judge (1Ma. 2:55) • Prophet (Sir. 46:1) • Savior (Sir. 46:1) • Intercessor (2Es. 7:107)	The New Testament calls Him: • Judge (Act. 10:42) • Prophet (Mat. 13:57) • Savior (Luk. 2:11) • Intercessor (Heb. 7:25)
Appointed 12 men to give witness to God's saving acts (Jos. 4:4-7)	Appointed 12 men to give witness to God's saving acts (Luk. 6:13; Act. 10:39-41)
Commander of God's earthly army (Jos. 1:10-11, 8:1)	Commander of God's heavenly army (Rev. 19:11-14; cf. Jos. 5:13-15)
Rescued the believing Gentiles (Jos. 6:22-25)	Rescued the believing Gentiles (Joh. 10:16. Act. 26:23)
His fame spread (Jos. 6:27)	His fame spread (Luk. 5:15)
Finished the work God gave him to do (Jos. 11:15)	Finished the work God gave Him to do (Joh. 17:4)
Left a large stone as witness (Jos. 24:26-27)	Left a large stone as witness (Mar. 16:4)
Gave a farewell address and	Gave a farewell address and

Appendices

Commissioned witnesses (Jos. 23:1-16, 24:22-23)

Commissioned witnesses (Mat. 28:16-20, Act. 1:8)

Made in the USA
Middletown, DE
02 April 2018